TOYS THAT SHOOT

With Values

Prof. James L. Dundas

Schiffer Publishing Ltd

4880 Lower Valley Rd. Atglen, PA 19310 USA

Library of Congress Catalog Card Number: 97-81352

Designed by Bonnie M. Hensley
Layout by Jerry Fronefield & Randy L. Hensley
Garamond

ISBN: 0-7643-0554-9
Printed in China
1 2 3 4

Published by Schiffer Publishing Ltd.
4880 Lower Valley Road
Atglen, PA 19310
Phone: (610) 593-1777; Fax: (610) 593-2002
E-mail: Schifferbk@aol.com
Please write for a free catalog.
This book may be purchased from the publisher.
Please include $3.95 for shipping.

Please try your bookstore first.

We are interested in hearing from authors
with book ideas on related subjects.

This book is dedicated to my brother, and all of those
brothers and sisters who were killed in Vietnam.

Brother

Only memories of you my brother have I left to ease the pain,
only memories as of sunshine that is banished by the rain.
With the autumn flowers you faded and with them have gone to rest.
Forgive me in my anguish, for perhaps thou knowest best.
All in vain I try to fathom why you went to Vietnam,
was your gallant soul concealing, what we know so well today?
That you were a true American and believe in the American way,
and now have gone away.
Winter's winds will sigh in mourning, spring will bring the flowers once more,
to embellish summer's grandeur, then to die at autumn's door.
Some day God will call to me, and I will set forth,
but perhaps it's a sunny morning and I will find a garden fair,
full of flowers and little children, and my Brother will be there.
Smiling he will come to meet me, and I think I hear him say.
"Did you say that you had missed me? Why I haven't been away."

For Sgt. Jerry R. Dundas
Killed at Khesanh, Vietnam on 5/5/68
from his brother Prof. James L. Dundas

Also dedicated

To my mother Dorothy Schillinger who threw away my childhood toys.
If she hadn't, I wouldn't have cared for old toys, and this book would not be.

And to my dear wife Janet M. Dundas who started my interest in old toys.

A very special thanks to the people at Century Camera Inc. of Royal Oak, Michigan,
for their help.

SAFE

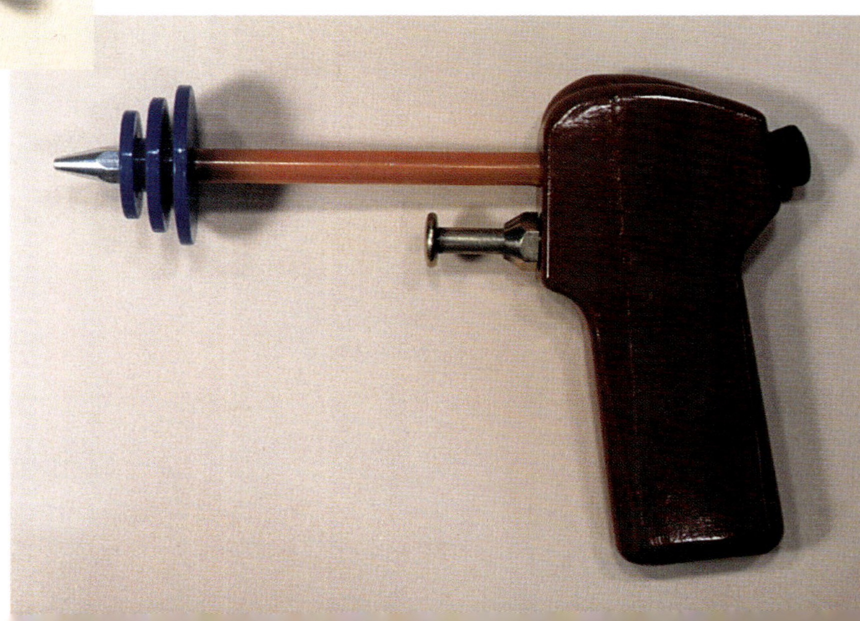

Contents

Preface 6

Chapter 1. History 7
- Daisy Manufacturing Company 7
- Chronology of Daisy BB guns 7
- Patent Numbers, Area Codes, and Zip Codes 9
- Dating Marked Objects From Japan 10

Chapter 2. Boy's Toys 11
- BB Guns 11
  - Pistols 11
  - Rifles 23
  - Daisy parts 31
  - Daisy collectibles 37
  - New Daisy rifles 39
- Candy shooters 41
- Cap shooters 42
- Cork shooters 56
- Dart shooters 61
- Marble shooters 66
- Ping pong shooters 67
- Key chain puzzles 70
- Rubber band shooters 81
- Squirt guns 83
- Things that shoot 104

Preface

People have been collecting BB guns for some time, but it is just in the last fifteen years or so that BB guns have gone way up in price and I think that they are going to remain expensive. What are the hottest models to collect? Those have to be the Daisy BB guns.

Of all the Daisy BB guns that have been made throughout the years, the most famous has to be the Red Ryder Carbine. Daisy designed the Red Ryder to hold many BBs and to shoot well. It had a fair amount of power and, not only did it look good to a kid, it was priced so that a kid could buy one.

The movie, *A Christmas Story*, set in the late 1940s, portrays a young boy's desire to get a Red Ryder BB gun for Christmas. When he is asked what he would like for Christmas he says, "I want a Red Ryder BB gun with a sun dial and a compass in the stock." His mother or most adults respond by telling him "you will shoot your eye out." Undaunted, he still plots ways to get this Red Ryder BB gun for Christmas. One small note about this wonderful movie, the Red Ryder Carbine that was made in the 1940s did not have a sun dial and a compass in the stock. The BB gun with a sun dial and a compass in the stock was the Model 107 Buck Jones, made by the Daisy Mfg. Co. Plymouth, Michigan from 1934 to 1940. Even though the movie has this small inaccurate statement, it is still a movie you must see.

There are more than BB guns that shoot, there are Candy shooters, Cap shooters, Cork shooters, Dart shooters, Marble shooters, Pea shooters, Ping Pong shooters, Rubber Band shooters and Squirt Guns.

That is not all—this book also includes key chain puzzles. You may wonder *why* I have included these puzzles in this particular book. Well, on those long car rides you could not play with the bigger toys ... certainly not shooting toys. For those times, these puzzles were great. At first you just took them apart and put them back together again. When that became easy, you took them apart again and did not look at them when you put them back together. That was the hard way. While you can still find these key chain puzzles for a good price if you search, they are starting to rise in price as they become harder to find. A nice thing about collecting key chain puzzles is that they do not take up much space.

All of these things were fun to play with when we were kids—and still may be for some. Its not just the collecting that may interest you but the money that you can make if you know what these items are worth.

This book was written to give you some idea of the types of BB guns—and other shooters—that were made, to provide tips on how to tell if some guns are original and if they work, and to provide information about how much these boy's toys are worth.

The prices in this book are the prices that I have personally sold toys for or have seen them sell for in the Midwest. Note that these prices may be doubled in California or New York. Prices vary immensely according to the condition of the piece, the location of the market, and the overall quality of the design and manufacture. Condition is always of paramount importance in assigning a price. As I stated, prices in the Midwest differ from those in the West or East, and those at specialty antique shows will vary from those at general shows. Of course, being in the right place at the right time can make all the difference.

All of these factors make it impossible to create an absolutely accurate price list; however, a useful general pricing guide can be offered. The values reflect what one might realistically expect to pay at retail or auction and are listed in U.S. dollars.

Prof. James L. Dundas
Macomb Community College
Warren, MI 48093

Chapter 1. History

Daisy Manufacturing Company, Plymouth, Michigan.

Daisy started out in the late 1800s as the Plymouth Iron Windmill Company, selling windmills to pump water. The windmill was named the "Daisy" because it looked like the daisy flower. Sales began to decline, and became bad enough the company almost went out of business. To boost sales, the Plymouth Iron Windmill Company began giving a free BB gun, "made by the King BB Gun Company," for children to play with, with every Daisy windmill purchased.

While windmill sales continued to fall, people wanted to buy those BB guns for their children. In fact, the BB guns caught on big, so big in fact that Daisy quit making windmills and bought the King BB Gun Company. On January 26, 1895, the BB gun was renamed the Daisy. Daisy BB guns were made in Plymouth, Michigan, from 1895 until 1958 when a fire burned down the factory. Daisy left Michigan and relocated in Rogers, Arkansas, where they still manufacture excellent BB guns today.

Chronology of Daisy BB guns

This chronology of Daisy BB guns was compiled by Daisy and is not 100% accurate. However, it will give you some idea of when the BB gun was made.

Model #	Made from	Type	Made of
1901	1901-1902	break action repeater	nickel plated
1901	1901-1902	lever action 500 shot	nickel plated
1903	1903-1904	lever action 1000 shot	nickel plated
3	1904-1909	lever action 500 shot	nickel plated
3	1910-1918	lever action 1000 shot	nickel plated
3	1919-1920	lever action 1000 shot	blued steel
3	1921-1934	lever action 1000 shot	nickel plated
3B	1914-1919	Daisy Special 1000 shot	blued steel
3B	1920-1922	Daisy Special 500 shot	blued steel
11	1917-1918	lever action 500 shot	nickel plated
11	1919-1921	lever action 350 shot	blued steel
11	1922-1937	lever action 350 shot	nickel plated
12	1918-1919	lever action single shot	nickel plated
12	1920-1933	lever action single shot	blued steel
12	1934-1937	lever action single shot	nickel or blued steel
20	1908-1911	Little Daisy single shot	nickel plated
20	1911-1919	break action repeater	nickel plated
20	1920-1931	break action repeater	blued steel
20	1932-1934	break action repeater	nickel plated
20	1935-1937	break action repeater	blued steel
21	1968-1070	Double Barrel 96 shot	painted steel
25	1914-1924	pump action repeater	blued-wooden stock
25	1925-1952	pump action repeater	blued-pistol grip stock
25	1953-1959	pump action repeater	painted-pistol grip stock
25	1960-1976	pump action, plastic stock	painted steel
25	1977-1995	new type of plastic stock	painted steel
25	1986-1987	Centennial replica.177	painted steel
26	1964-1967	Field Master Slide Action	painted steel
27	1916-1917	lever action 500 shot	blued steel
27	1918-1919	lever action 500 shot	nickel plated
27	1919-1935	lever action 500 shot	blued steel
30	1915-1917	lever action 500 shot	bronze
33	1949-1951	Cub 500 shot	nickel plate
33	1952-1953	Cub 350 shot	blued steel
33	1953-1955	Cub 350 shot	painted steel
36	1936-1950	lever action single shot	blued steel
36	1936-1951	Cub 500 shot	nickel plate
40	1916-1930	lever action military	blued steel
50	1936-1949	Daisy Golden Eagle	Copper
62	1975-1978	Target Spring Air .177 Pellet	painted steel
65	1968-1978	FWB Pellet Pistol .177 Cal.	painted steel
70	1976-1977	Safari Mark 1 Magnet Feed	painted steel
75	1953-1954	Scout Rifle 500 shot	blued steel
75	1954-1955	Scout Rifle 500 shot	painted steel
80	1955-1956	Long Rifle 1000 shot	painted steel
86	1970-1975	Safari Mark 1 240 shot	painted steel
88	1961-1962	Hunter Air Rifle 2 X Scope	painted steel
90	1973-1974	700 shot with safety	painted steel
92	1986-1987	10 shot pistol.177	
94	1955-1962	Red Ryder Carbine 1000 Shot	painted steel
95 A	1962-1976	700 Shot	painted steel
95 B	1977-1989	Magnet feed	painted steel
96	1963-1973	700 Shot	painted steel
97	1961-1962	Saddle Gun Ricochet 650 shot	painted steel
98	1955-1961	Daisy Eagle 2X Scope	painted steel
98	1974-1975	700 Shot Plastic Stock	painted steel
98	1975-1976	700 Shot wood Stock	painted steel
98	1976-1978	Wood Stock Magnetic Feed	painted steel
98	1979-1981	Monte Carlo target	painted steel
99	1961-1978	Target Special	painted steel
99 A	1979-1980	Target Special	painted steel
99 B	1980-1984	Target Special	painted steel
100	1962-1963	CO2 Semi-Automatic Pistol	painted steel

Model #	Made from	Type	Made of
101	1933-1935	lever action single shot	blued steel
102	1933-1935	Cub 500 shot	nickel plated
102	1960-1978	Cub 500 Shot	painted steel
103	1959-1962	Scout	painted steel
103	1933-1936	Buzz Barton super 1000 shot	nickel plate
103	1953-1955	Buzz Barton super 1000 shot	painted steel
103	1963-1965	Scout 700 Shot	painted steel
104	1939-1940	Double Barrel	blued steel
104	1966-1972	Golden Eagle Peep Sight	painted steel
104	1973-1978	Golden Eagle with Safty	painted steel
105	1933-1934	Junior Pump Gun	blued steel
105 A	1979-1980	Cub 500 Shot	painted steel
105 B	1980-1989	Cub 500 Shot	painted steel
105	1984-1985	Pal 400 shot .177 Cal.	painted steel
106	1955-1957	Break action 500 Shot	painted steel
107	1959-1962	Slide Action 30 Shot	painted steel
107	1934-1942	Buck Jones Sundial Compass	blued steel
108	1936-1942	Lightning Loader Mod. 39	blued steel
110	1968-1969	FWB Match Rifle .177 Cal.	painted steel
111	1938-1952	Red Ryder Carbine Mod. 40	blued steel
111	1953-1955	Red Ryder Carbine Mod. 40	painted steel
111	1963-1978	Red Ryder Plastic Stock	painted steel
111 A	1979-1980	Red Ryder Plastic Stock	painted steel
111 B	1980-1989	Red Ryder Plastic Stock	painted steel
118	1937-1938	Targeteer Pistol .118 Cal.	nickel plate
118	1939-1952	Targeteer Pistol .118 Cal.	blued steel
120	1984-1985	Break barrel pellet .177 Cal.	painted steel
126	1984-1985	EL Gamo Pneumatic .177 Cal.	painted steel
130	1986-1987	Auto pellet 25 shot .177 Cal.	painted steel
140	1942-1943	Defender Military 1000 Shot	blued steel
141	1952-1953	Defender New Daisy Repeater	blued steel
142	1953-1955	Defender New Daisy Repeater	painted steel
150	1968-1969	FWB Match Rifle .177 Cal.	painted steel
155	1946-1952	lever action 1000 shot	blued steel
155	1953-1954	lever action 1000 shot	painted
160	1965-1975	BB-Pellet- Dart Rifle .177 Cal.	painted steel
177	1957-1959	Bulleye Pistol 150 Shot BB	painted steel
179	1960-1982	Peace maker revolver 12 Shot	painted steel
188	1979-1989	BB pellet pistol	painted steel
195	1933-1934	Buzz Barton Special	nickel plate
195	1935-1940	Buzz Barton Special	blued steel
200	1963-1976	CO2 Semi-Automatic Pistol	painted steel
220	1965-1972	Pellet Rifle .177 Cal.	painted steel
225	1973-1974	Pellet Rifle .177 Cal.	painted steel
230	1965-1974	Pellet Rifle .22 Cal.	painted steel

Model #	Made from	Type	Made of
250	1965-1974	Pellet Rifle .22 Cal.	painted steel
300	1968-1975	CO2 Semi-Auto. 500 Shot	painted steel
400	1971-1972	5 Shot Pellet	painted steel
404	1973-1976	5 Shot Pellet	painted steel
440	1967-1968	Match Maker .177 Cal. Pellet	painted steel
450	1971-1972	5 Shot Pellet	painted steel
454	1973-1976	5 Shot Pellet	painted steel
460	1967-1968	Match Maker .22 Cal. Pellet	painted steel
499	1976-1979	Target single shot	painted steel
499A	1980-1981	Target single shot	painted steel
499B	1981-1989	Target single shot	painted steel
572	1968-1971	Field Master Slide Action	painted steel
717	1979-1985	Pneumatic single pump target	painted steel
722	1986-1989	Pneumatic single pump target	painted steel
770	1974-1978	Super Spring Air	painted steel
777	1981-1989	Pneumatic single pump target	painted steel
780	1981-1982	CO2 Pellet pistol	painted steel
790	1982-1983	CO2 Pellet pistol	painted steel
822	1976-1989	Pneumatic Pellet .22 Cal.	painted steel
836	1984-1985	Powerline BB Pellet .177 Cal.	painted steel
840	1978-1989	Single pump BB or Pellet	painted steel
845	1980-1989	840 target with peep sights	painted steel
850	1982-1983	BB-Pellet .177 Cal.	painted steel
851	1983-1984	BB-Pellet .177 Cal.	painted steel
853	1984-1985	Pneumatic single pump .177 Cal.	painted steel
860	1984-1985	Powerline BB Pellet .177 Cal.	painted steel
880	1972-1990	Pneumatic BB and pellet	painted steel
881	1973-1983	880 With Rifled Barrel	painted steel
882	1975-1976	880 Target with peep sight	painted steel
856	1985-1986	Multipump BB pellet .177 Cal.	painted steel
900	1986-1987	Snap shot auto clip .177 Cal.	painted steel
917	1979-1982	Pneumatic multistroke 5 Shot	painted steel
922	1978-1989	Pneumatic multistroke 5 Shot	painted steel
953	1984-1985	U.S. Shooting team	painted steel
977	1980-1983	880 Target with peep sight	painted steel
977	1975-1986	Jaycee Program .177 Cal.	painted steel
1105	1975-1978	500 Shot with safety	painted steel
1200	1977-1989	CO2 60 shot BB	painted steel
1205	1979-1981	CO2 60 shot BB	painted steel
1770	1978-1980	Spring Air .177 Cal.	painted steel
1776	1968-1972	Golden Eagle Peep Sight	painted steel
1880	1978-1980	880 with scope	painted steel
1881	1978-1980	Powerline BB Pellet	painted steel
1894	1961-1986	Western Carbine 45 Shot	painted steel
1901	1901-1902	Break action repeater	nickel plated
1901	1901-1902	lever action 500 shot	nickel plated
1903	1903-1910	lever action 1000 shot	nickel plated

Model #	Made from	Type	Made of
1917	1978-1980	Powerline 5 shot clip .177 Cal.	painted steel
1922	1978-1980	Powerline Pneumatic .22 Cal.	painted steel
1938	1972-1978	Red Ryder Carbine Replica	painted steel
1938A	1979-1980	Red Ryder Carbine Replica	painted steel
1938B	1980-1995	Red Ryder Carbine Replica	painted steel
2299	1968-1976	Quick Skill	painted steel
2856	1985-1986	856 with 800 point sight	painted steel
2860	1984-1985	860 with 800 point scope	painted steel
3030	1969-1973	Carbine Buffalo Bill 45 Shot	painted steel
4300	1970-1974	FWB Match Rifle .177 Cal.	painted steel
4301	1975-1978	FWB Match Rifle .177 Cal.	painted steel
4301	1978-1979	Feinwerkbau single shot	painted steel
5179	1971-1972	NRA Centennial Commemorative	painted steel
5179	1973-1974	NRA Centennial Texas Rangers	painted steel
5179	1974-1975	NRA Centennial Wells Fargo	painted steel
5894	1971-1975	NRA Centennial Commemorative	painted steel
9052	1968-1981	Carbine Octagon Barrel-Sears	painted steel
97741	1980-1983	880 Target with peep sight	painted steel
A	1907-1908	Single shot	nickel plated
A	1908-1911	Break action repeater	nickel plated
C	1913-1915	Break action repeater	nickel plated
H	1913-1915	lever action single shot	blued steel
H	1916-1917	lever action 500 shot	nickel plated
VL	1968-1969	Caseless 22 Cal. single shot	painted steel

Patent Numbers, Area Codes, and Zip Codes

Patent Numbers can be a great help in telling how old an object is. If a patent number is greater than 2,185,170, then the object can date no earlier than 1940. Keep in mind that the object may still be made today, but usually not. A patent number expires after 17 years.

Patent Numbers and Dates

DATE	Patent #	DATE	Patent #	DATE	Patent #	DATE	Patent #	DATE	Patent #	DATE	Patent #
1836	1	1864	41047	1892	466315	1920	1326899	1948	2433824	1976	3930271
1837	110	1865	45685	1893	483976	1921	1354054	1949	2457797	1977	4000520
1838	546	1866	51784	1894	511744	1922	1401948	1950	2492944	1978	4065812
1839	1061	1867	60658	1895	531619	1923	1440352	1951	2536016	1979	4131952
1840	1465	1868	72959	1896	552502	1924	1478996	1952	2580379	1980	4180876
1841	1923	1869	85503	1897	574369	1925	1521590	1953	2624046	1981	4242757
1842	2413	1870	98460	1898	596467	1926	1568040	1954	2664562	1982	4308622
1843	2901	1871	110617	1899	616871	1927	1612700	1955	2698434	1983	4366579
1844	3395	1872	122304	1900	640167	1928	1654521	1956	2728913	1984	4423523
1845	3873	1873	134504	1901	664827	1929	1696897	1957	2775762	1985	4490885
1846	4348	1874	146120	1902	690385	1930	1742181	1958	2818567	1986	4562596
1847	4914	1875	158350	1903	717521	1931	1787424	1959	2868973	1987	4633526
1848	5409	1876	171641	1904	758567	1932	1839190	1960	2919443	1988	4716594
1849	5993	1877	185813	1905	778834	1933	1892663	1961	2966681	1989	4794652
1850	6961	1878	198753	1906	808618	1934	1941449	1962	3015103	1990	4890335
1851	7865	1879	211078	1907	839799	1935	1985678	1963	3070801	1991	4980927
1852	8622	1880	223211	1908	875679	1936	2026516	1964	3116487	1992	5077836
1853	9512	1881	236137	1909	908430	1937	2066309	1965	3163365		
1854	10358	1882	251685	1910	945010	1938	2104004	1966	3226729		
1855	12117	1883	269320	1911	980178	1939	2142080	1967	3295143		
1856	14009	1884	291016	1912	1013095	1940	2185170	1968	3360800		
1857	16324	1885	310163	1913	1049326	1941	2227418	1969	3419907		
1858	19010	1886	333494	1914	1083267	1942	2268540	1970	3487470		
1859	22477	1887	355291	1915	1125212	1943	2307007	1971	3551909		
1860	26642	1888	375720	1916	1166419	1944	2338061	1972	3633214		
1861	31005	1889	395305	1917	1210389	1945	2366154	1973	3707729		
1862	34045	1890	418655	1918	1251458	1946	2391856	1974	3781914		
1863	37266	1891	443987	1919	1290027	1947	2413675	1975	3858241		

Area Codes and Zip Codes

Another way to tell the age of an object is by whether or not it has an area code. Mr Walker, the postmaster in New York, introduced a two number area code for large cities on May 6, 1943. The area code numbering was stopped when they put zip codes on the mail. The five number zip codes started on July 1, 1963. In October 1984, Zip + four came into being; this improved zip code has the five number zip code plus four more numbers.

If an object has no area or zip code, then it may be older than May 6, 1943. However, in a town or city that had only one post office from 1943 to 1963 there were no two number area or zip codes.

So if you have something with a two number area code, then it was made from 1943 to 1963. If it has a zip code then it was made from 1963 to 1984. If you have something with five numbers, a dash, and four additional numbers, it can be no older than October 1984.

When you find the words "Made in Japan" printed on something, then it was made from 1921 to 1942 and maybe to the end of World War II in August 1945. If you find "Occupied Japan" printed on something, then it was made from 1945 to 1952. Japan was occupied by the U.S. Army at the end of World War II, from late August 1945 to April 28, 1952.

Here are some examples:

John Doe Toys
123 Main Street
Detroit, Mich.
It may be older than May 6, 1943.

John Doe Toys
123 Main Street
Detroit 09 Mich.
It was made from 1943 to 1963.

John Doe Toys
123 Main Street
Detroit, Mi. 48207
It was made from 1963 to 1984.

John Doe Toys
123 Main Street
Detroit, MI 48207 - 1144
It was made from 1984 to Date.

Dating Marked Objects from Japan

Item is marked Nippon: 1889 to 1919
Item is marked Japan: 1900 to 1919
Item is marked Made in Japan: 1919 to 1945
Item is marked Made in Norahocky: 1919 to 1945
Item is marked Made in Occupied Japan: 1946 to 1952

Chapter 2. Boy's Toys

BB Guns — Pistols

Daisy Targeteer target box, 11 3/4" x 6" x 3". $80-100.

Daisy targeteer table top plastic target, with nickel plated targeteer BB gun with adjustable rear sight, caliber 118, came with two tin tubes of BBs (either copper coated steel, copper, or #6 lead shot). This model is very hard to find. $600-700.

Daisy targeteer nickel plated caliber 118 BB gun with an adjustable rear sight, 10" long. Made from 1937 to 1952. $200-300.

Daisy targeteer target box, 10" x 1" x 5 1/4". Box only: $60-80.

Daisy targeteer target with target spinner, targets, BBs, and blued steel targeteer BB gun with fixed rear sight, caliber 118. Made from 1937 to 1952. $300-350.

Daisy targeteer blued steel BB gun with adjustable rear sight, caliber 118. Made from 1937 to 1952. $150-175.

Daisy targeteer blued steel BB gun with fixed rear sight, caliber 118. Made from 1937 to 1952. $125-150.

Wham-O BB Pistol box with original darts, BBs, caps, cleaner rod and loader rod, and instructions. Box only: $50-75.

Wham-O BB Pistol, 8" long x 4 3/4" high x 1 3/8" wide. Original box. This pistol came with a package of BBs, two darts, and a ramrod. To load the gun, cock the bolt by pulling it back to the lock position. Place one or two caps with the red side facing forward in the breech. To insure maximum firing power, be sure that the power portion of the cap is in line with the opening of the barrel with the narrow edge of the cap down. To load, tilt the barrel up and drop one BB down the barrel. Made of styrene plastic with a steel barrel by the Wham-O Manufacturing Co. 835 E. El Monte St., San Gabriel, California, in 1954. Sold for $2.98. $250- $350.

Benjamin Franklin first pneumatic air pistol, model 100, single shot BB with push-rod Pump on end of barrel, 10" long with a fixed rear sight. Made of blued brass with wooden grips in the 1930s. $350 to $450.

Benjamin Franklin first model pneumatic air pistol, model 107, single shot BB with push-rod pump on end of barrel, 10" long with a fixed rear sight. Made of nickel plated brass with wooden grips in the 1930s. $350 to $450.

Benjamin Franklin second model pneumatic air pistol, model 117, single shot BB with swinging lever pump on end of barrel, 10" long with adjustable rear sight. Made of blued brass with wooden grips in the 1940s. $250 to $350.

Benjamin Franklin third model pneumatic air pistol, model 137, single shot BB with short stroke pump rod lever on end of barrel, 11" long with adjustable rear sight. Made of blued brass with wooden grips in the 1950s. $200 to $300.

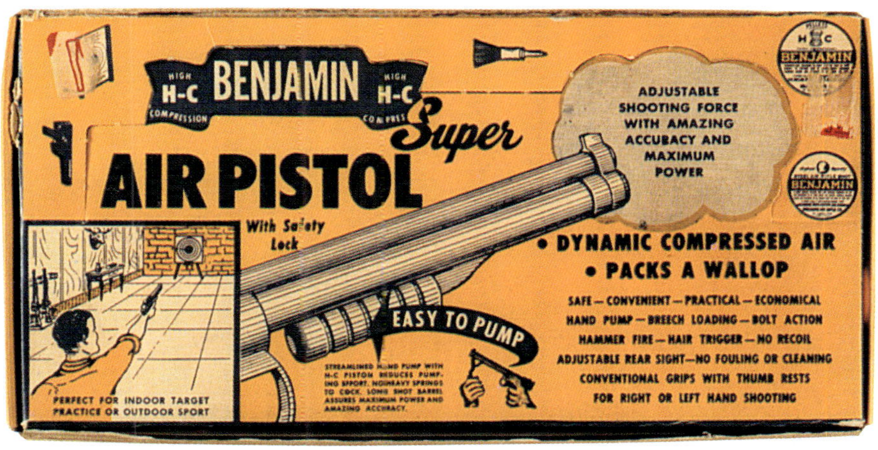

Benjamin Franklin third model pneumatic air pistol, model 137 box. The box measures 11 1/2" x 6" x 1". Made in the 1960s. Box only: $30-40.

Benjamin Franklin third model pneumatic air pistol, model 137, single shot BB with short stroke pump rod lever on end of barrel, 11" long with adjustable rear sight. Made of blued brass with plastic grips in the 1960s. $100 to $150.

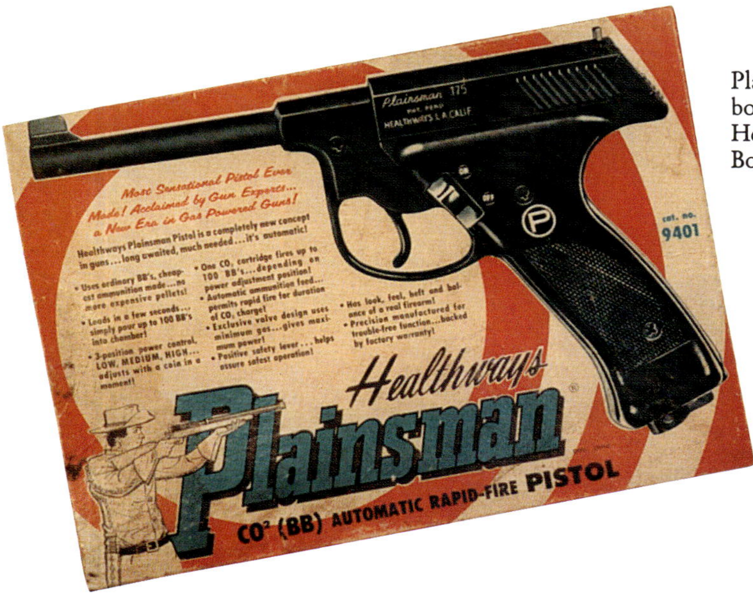

Plainsman BB gun original box, 11" x 8" x 2". Made by Healthways in the 1960s. Box only: $30-40.

Plainsman CO2 Automatic BB Gun by Healthways, in the original box. This gun takes a short CO2 cylinder measuring 2 1/2" long, not the newer 3 1/4 " long cylinder. Made in the 1960s. $150-200.

Marksman BB pistol, 8" long single shot. Made by Morton H. Harris of Los Angeles, California, in the 1950s. $60-80.

Rogers Automatic BB Gun, takes a 3 1/4" long CO2 cylinder. Made in the 1970s. $60-80.

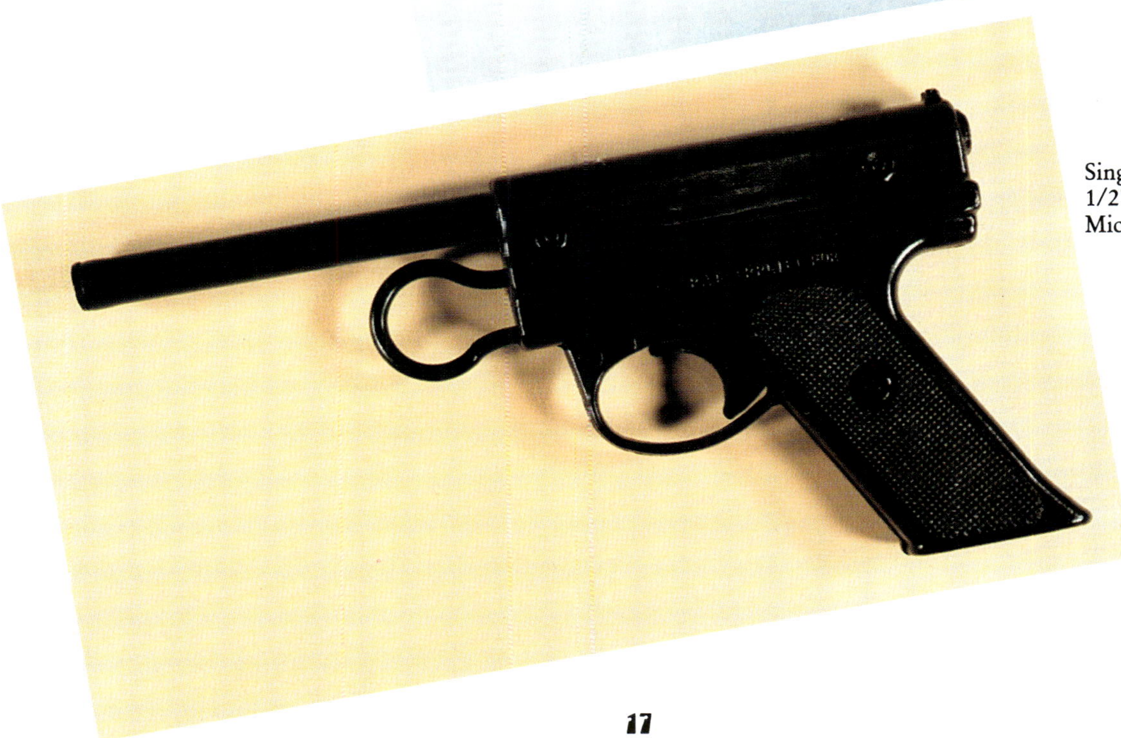

Single shot BB gun, 9 1/2" long. Made in Michigan. $30-40.

The Haig pistol is a BB gun and a cap gun. It is made of plastic with a steel barrel. The barrel alone is 9 3/4" long, and the gun overall is of 13 1/2" long. The Haig shoots lead bullets — .12 Cal. or # 6 bird shot is used. To load the gun, cock the hammer by pulling back to the lock position, then tilt the barrel up and drop one bullet down the barrel. Place one or two caps in the breech and shoot. The caps used are the page type caps rather than the roll type. The Haig was sold for $3.00 and was made in the 1960s by Haig Mfg. Co., P.O. Box 24-B, Alhambra, Cal 91802. Also sold as style # 7211 by the Wham-O Manufacturing Co., Dep AR 3835 E, El Monte St., San Gabriel, California 91778, and sold for $2.95 in 1965. $100-150.

Daisy targeteer BB shot, caliber 118, 1 7/8" x 3/4". There are three types of shot: copper coated steel, copper, and # 6 lead shot. The copper coated steel and the copper came in the same tube "Tint BBs." The only way to tell what type you have is with a magnet. Daisy started out using the copper coated steel then went to copper BBs for the targeteer. Later this proved to be too costly and they went to the # 6 lead shot which was cheaper but it did not shoot very far. A tube of all copper coated steel is worth $20-25; a tube of all copper is worth $15-20; and a tube of all # 6 lead is worth $10-15.

Single shot BB gun, prize found in a box of Cracker Jack. 1 1/2" long. Made of die cast metal in Japan in 1910. $40-50.

Larc International model M19-A BB Machine Gun BB gun, 20" long, made of plastic. It holds 5000 BBs and is propelled by Refrigerant R-12 gas. This was a fun gun to shoot. You can use compressed air at a pressure of not more than 100 pounds. Made in the 1970s. Very hard to find. $150-200.

Daisy 500 targeteer shot, caliber 118, 2 1/4" x 3/4". The BBs are copper coated steel. The caliber 118 copper coated steel are the hardest to find. $25-30.

Daisy Power Line 1700 60 shot CO2 BB repeater, 11" long. Made in the 1990s. $40-50.

Daisy mode 288 air pistol 24 shot BB repeater, 11 3/4" long. Made in the 1990s. $40-50.

Daisy Power Line 400 semiauto CO2 BB repeater, 10 1/2" long. Made in the 1990s. $40-50.

Daisy Power Line 44 .177 Cal. CO2 BB six shot, 12" long. Made in the 1990s. $40-50.

Daisy Power Line 500 .177 Cal. CO2 BB single shot, 8 3/4" long. Made in the 1990s. $40-50.

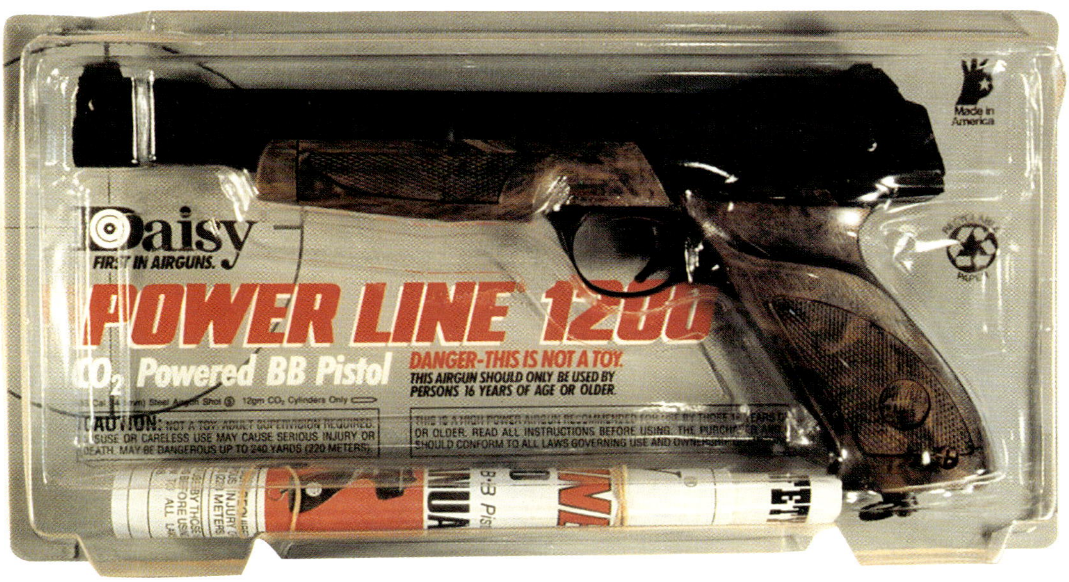

Daisy Power Line 1200 CO2 BB, 11 1/2" long. Made in the 1990s. $40-50.

Daisy Power Line 45, 13 shot CO2 pellet repeater, 8 1/2" long. Made with a blued finish in the 1990s. $40-50.

Daisy Power Line 45, 13 shot CO2 pellet repeater, 8 1/2" long. Made with a chrome finish in the 1990s. $40-50.

Daisy Power Line 93, 15 shot BB repeater, 8" long. Made with a blued finish in the 1990s. $40-50.

Daisy Power Line 93, 15 shot BB repeater, 8" long. Made with a chrome finish in the 1990s. $40-50.

Daisy model 188, 24 shot repeater, 11 1/2" long. Made in the 1990s. $40-50.

Number 27 Daisy lever action 500 shot blued steel with a cast iron lever and wooden stock. BB loaded in top 3/16" opening, overall length of 32". Made from 1916 to 1917. $150-200.

Number 27 Daisy lever action 500 shot blued steel with a cast iron lever and wooden stock, BB loaded in top 5/16" opening, has an overall length of 32". Made from 1916 to 1917. $150-200.

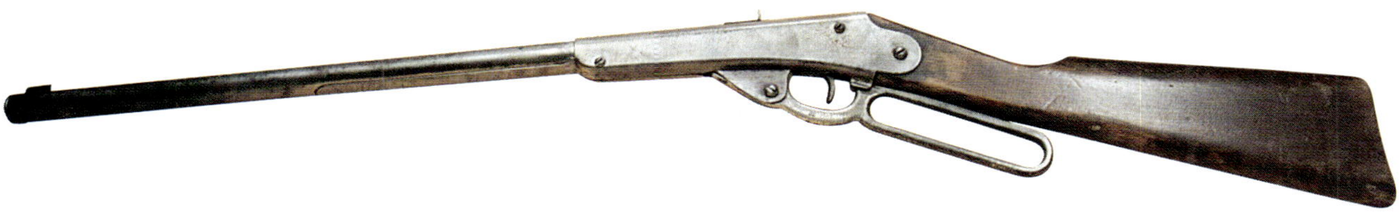

Number 27 Daisy lever action 1000 shot blued steel with a cast iron lever and wooden stock, BB loaded in top 3/16" opening, has an overall length of 32". Made from 1916 to 1917. $175-225.

Model 29 Number 11 Daisy lever action 350 shot nickel plated with a cast iron lever and wooden stock. BB loaded in top 3/16" opening, has an overall length of 31". Made from 1919 to 1921. $150-200.

Model 33 number 102 Daisy, 500 shot with a cast iron lever and wooden stock, overall length of 31", side load opening 3/16". Made from 1936 to 1948. $175-225.

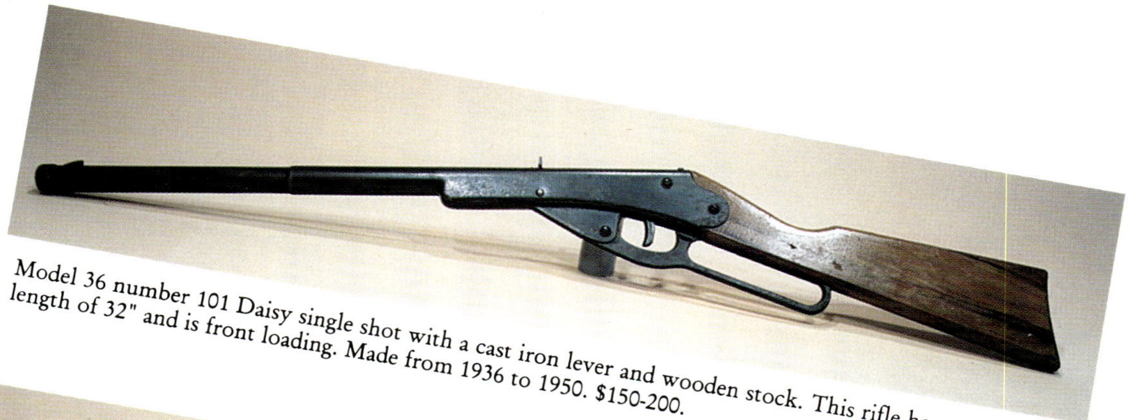

Model 36 number 101 Daisy single shot with a cast iron lever and wooden stock. This rifle has an overall length of 32" and is front loading. Made from 1936 to 1950. $150-200.

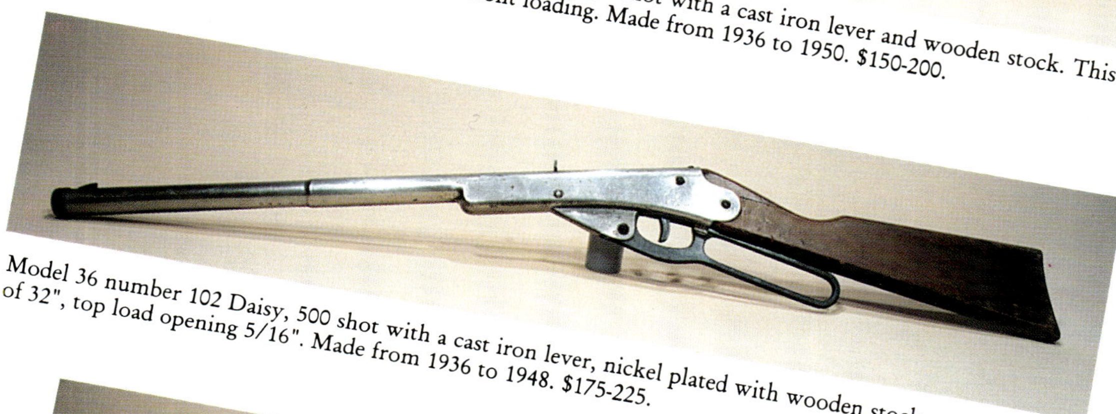

Model 36 number 102 Daisy, 500 shot with a cast iron lever, nickel plated with wooden stock, overall length of 32", top load opening 5/16". Made from 1936 to 1948. $175-225.

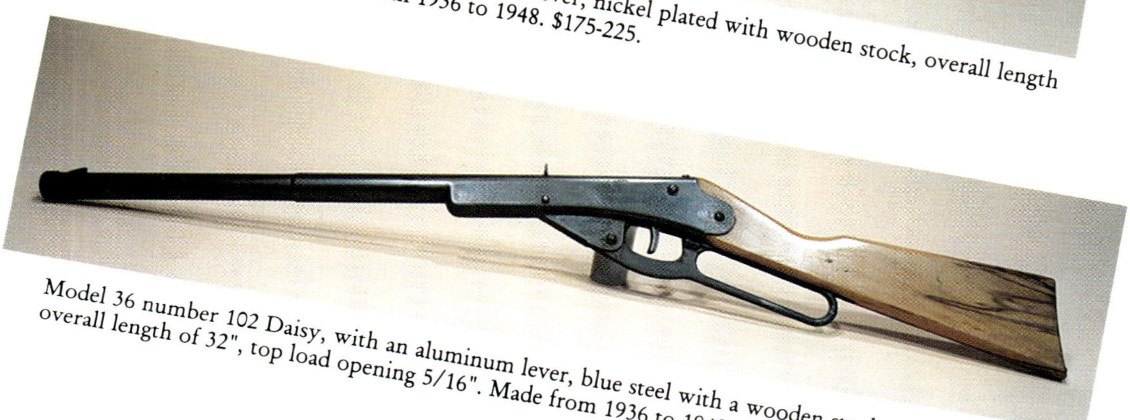

Model 36 number 102 Daisy, with an aluminum lever, blue steel with a wooden stock, overall length of 32", top load opening 5/16". Made from 1936 to 1948. $150-200.

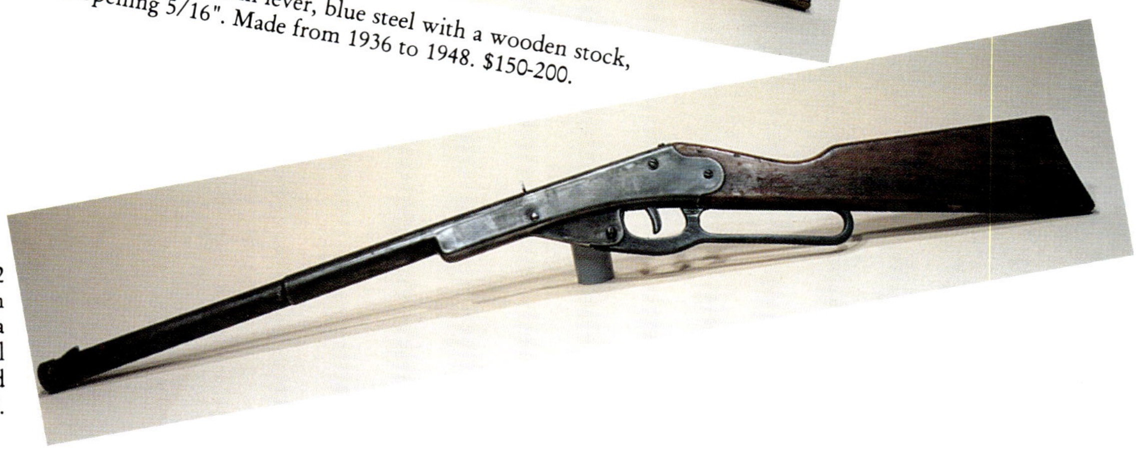

Model 36 number 102 Daisy, 500 shot cast iron lever, blue steel with a wooden stock, overall length of 32", top load opening 3/16". $150-200.

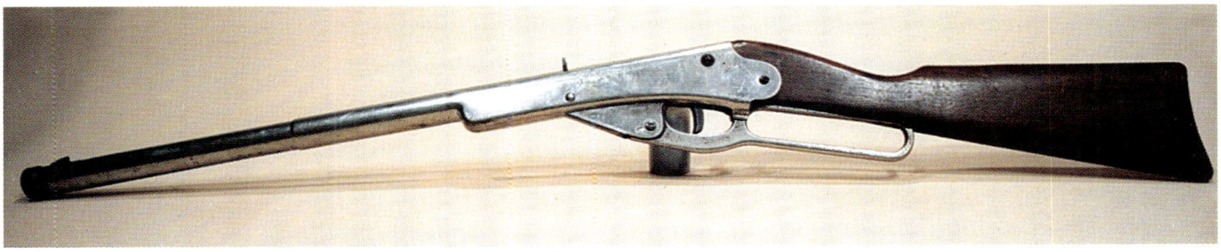

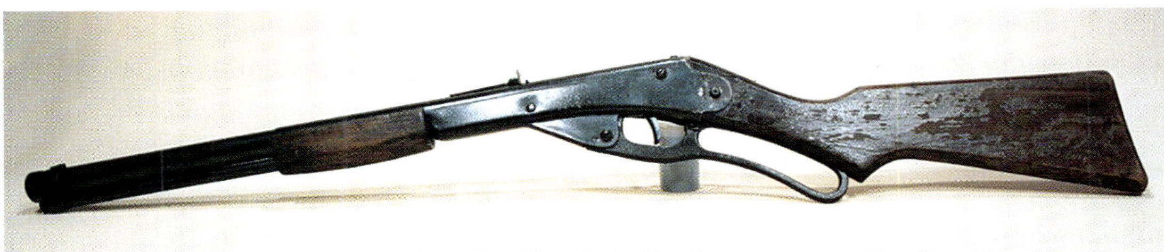

From top to bottom:
Model 36 number 102 Daisy, 500 shot with a nickel plated cast iron lever, nickel plated with a wooden stock, overall length of 33 1/4", top load opening 3/16". $200-250.

Model 36 number 102 Daisy, 500 shot cast iron lever, blue steel with a wooden stock, overall length of 32", top load 5/16" opening. $150-200.

Model 38 number #100 Daisy, single shot with a wooden stock, overall length of 31 1/4", front loading. $150-200.

Model # 39 Number 108 Daisy Lightning Loader. It has a wooden forearm and stock, is made of blued steel with a cast iron lever. The overall length is 33". This is the basic design that the Red Ryder was made from. Made from 1936 to 1942. $150-200.

Number 40 Daisy military lever action, blued steel with a cast iron lever and wooden stock, overall length of 36 1/2 inches. Made from 1916 to 1930. Hard to find. $250-300.

From top to bottom:
Model 75 Scout, 31 3/4" long. Aluminum lever plastic forearm and stock. $70-80.

Number 195 model 36 Daisy Buzz Barton Special, blued steel with a cast iron lever and wooden stock, overall length of 35", top load 5/16". Made from 1933 to 1940. $250-300.

Number 195 model 36 Daisy Buzz Barton Special, blued steel with a cast iron lever and wooden stock, overall length of 35", top load 3/16". Made from 1933 to 1940. $250-300.

Number 103 Daisy Buzz Barton Super Special, 1000 shot nickel plated with a cast iron lever, wooden stock, and a rear sight. Note: the rear sight is missing from this gun. The overall length is 35 1/2". Made from 1933 to 1936. $300-350.

Number 111 Daisy Red Ryder Carbine Model #40. It has a wooden forearm and stock, is made of blued steel with a cast iron lever, and an adjustable rear sight. "Red Ryder" is branded on the stock. You must be able to read "Red Ryder" on the stock when the barrel is pointing to the left for it to be an original stock. Overall length of 35 1/2". Made from 1938 to 1942. $200-250.

Number 111 Daisy Red Ryder Carbine Model #40. The 1941 model with copper bands, a wooden forearm and stock. It was made of blued steel with a cast iron lever, an adjustable rear sight, and has an overall length of 35 1/2 ". Made in 1941. Hard to find. $250-300.

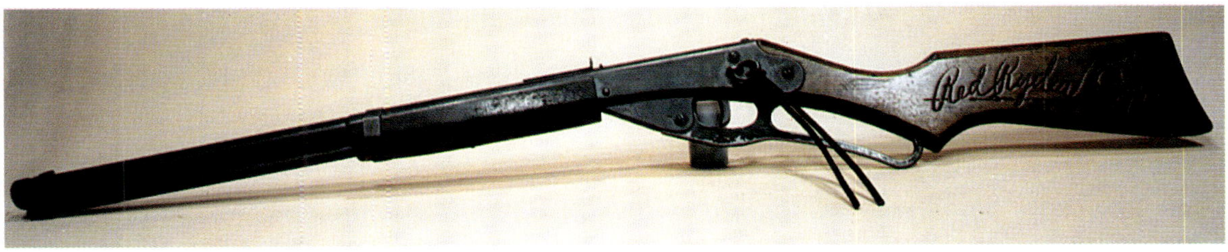

Number 111 Daisy Red Ryder Carbine Model #40. It has a wooden forearm and stock, was made of blued steel with an aluminum lever with a fixed rear sight, and it has "Red Ryder" branded in on the stock. Overall length of 35 1/2". Made from 1942 to 1958. $150-200.

Original Red Ryder box. Very hard to find. $100-150.

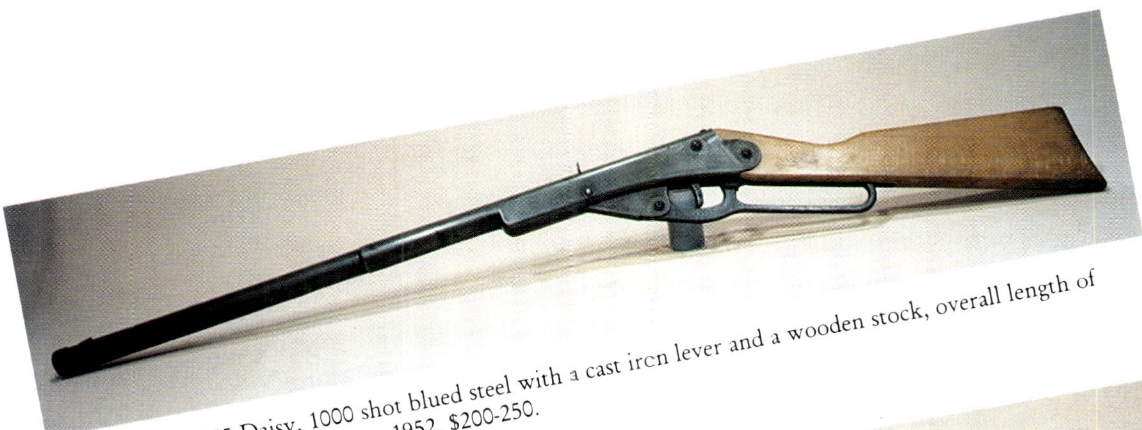

Number 155 Daisy, 1000 shot blued steel with a cast iron lever and a wooden stock, overall length of 34 1/2". Made from 1946 to 1952. $200-250.

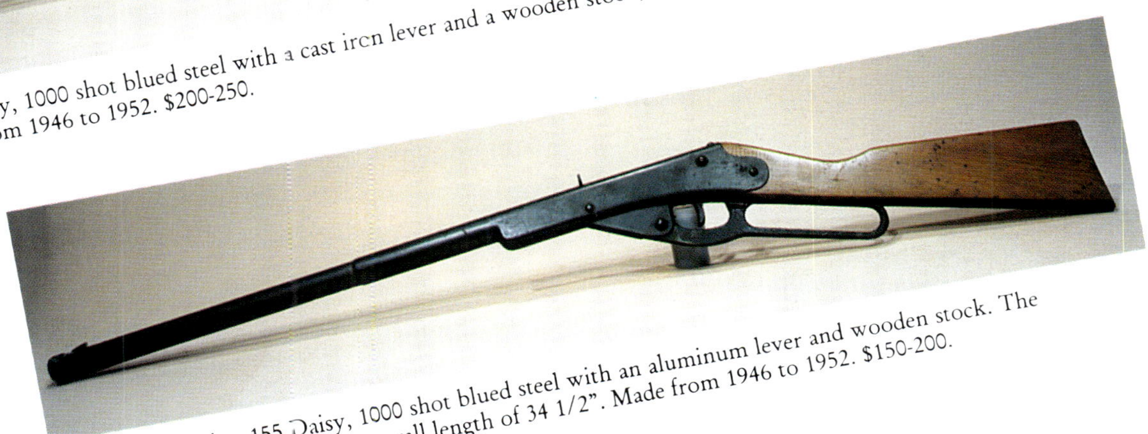

Number 155 Daisy, 1000 shot blued steel with an aluminum lever and wooden stock. The Number 155 has an overall length of 34 1/2". Made from 1946 to 1952. $150-200.

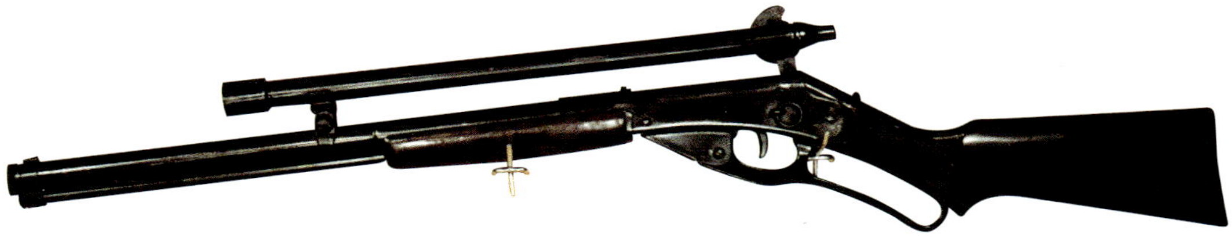

Model 75 Daisy with a 2 X scope, painted steel with a plastic forearm and stock. It has an overall length of 36". $150-200.

Daisy JC Higgins Cactus Carbine by Sears and Roebuck. It has a plastic forearm and stock and measures 31 1/2" long. Hard to find. $200-300.

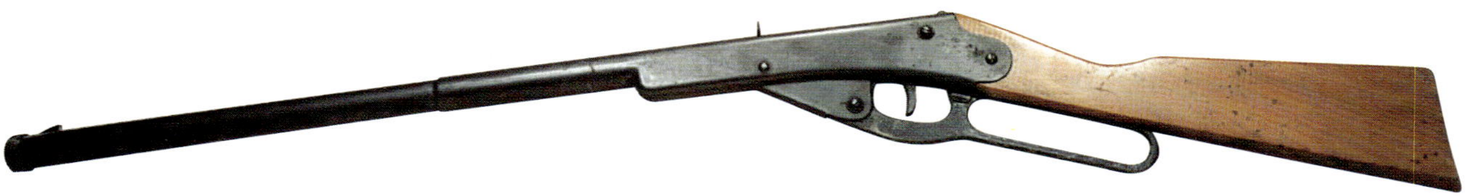

Number 98 Daisy Eagle, painted steel with plastic forearm and stock, adjustable rear sight, and an overall length of 36". Made circa 1958. $100-150.

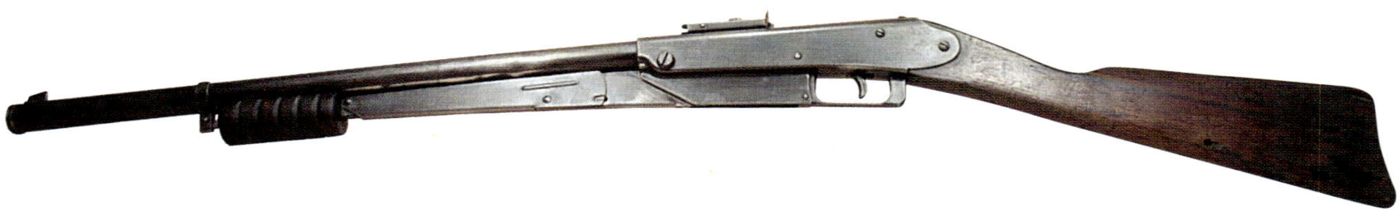

Number 25 Daisy Pump Action Repeater 50 Shot Force Feed. The 1915 Model is made of blued steel with a wooden forearm and stock, and has an overall length of 36 3/4". $250-350.

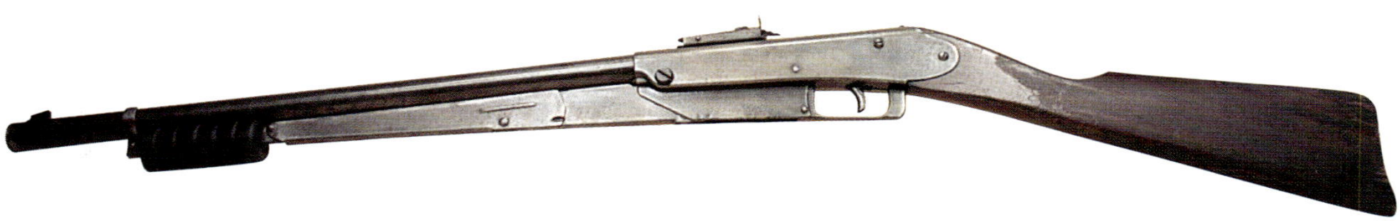

Number 25 Daisy pump action repeater, 50 Shot Force Feed. The 1920 model is made of blued steel with a wooden forearm and stock, and has an overall length of 36 3/4". $200-250.

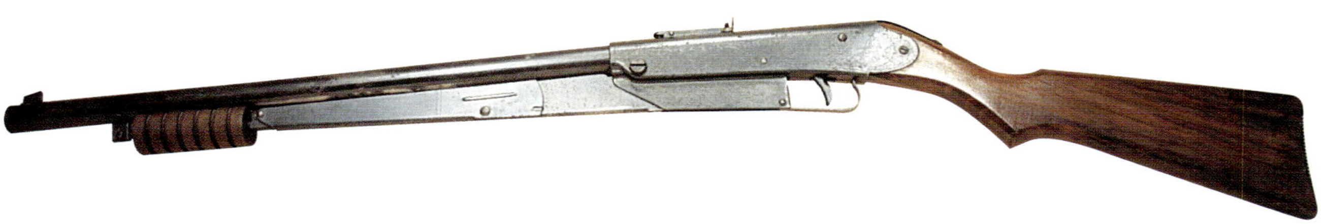

Number 25 Daisy Pump 50 Shot Force Feed pistol grip stock. Made with a wooden, gum, or birch forearm and stock from 1936 to 1941. $150-200.

Top to bottom:
Number 25 Daisy Pump 50 Shot Force Feed, wooden forearm with a plastic stock. Made in 1958. $80-90.

Number 25 Daisy Pump 50 Shot Force Feed, plastic forearm and a plastic stock. Made in 1958. $60-80.

Number 25 Daisy Pump 50 Shot Force Feed, plastic forearm and a plastic stock. Made in 1995. $30-35.

Model 104 Double Barrel, two 50 Shot Force Feed shot tubes. Made of blued steel with a wooden forearm and stock, 38" long. Made in 1938. Very rare. $1200-1500.

Model 104 Double Barrel top.

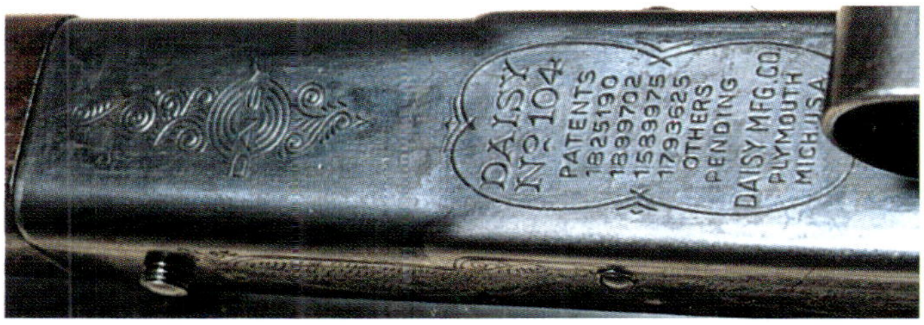

Model 104 Double Barrel bottom.

Number #107 Daisy Buck Jones Special Pump slide action rifle, blued steel, 60 shot with a sundial and compass on a wooden stock. This rifle has an overall length of 36 1/2". Made from 1934 to 1942. $250-350.

Number #107 Daisy Buck Jones Special.

Number #107 Buck Jones sundial and compass.

Benjamin Franklin pneumatic air rifle, model 300, single shot BB or pellet with an air pump on the end of the barrel. Made of brass with a wooden stock and measuring 34 1/2" long with a fixed rear sight. Made in the 1930s. $300-400.

Benjamin Franklin pneumatic air rifle, model 300, single shot BB or pellet with an air pump on the end of the barrel. Made of blued brass with a wooden stock and measuring 34 1/2" long with a fixed rear sight. Made in the 1930s. $300-400.

Benjamin Franklin pneumatic air rifle, model 340, single shot BB or pellet with a lever air pump. Made of blued brass with a wooden stock. $200-250.

Benjamin Franklin pneumatic air rifle, model 312, single shot .22 Cal. pellet with a lever air pump. Made of nickel plated brass with a wooden stock. $200-250.

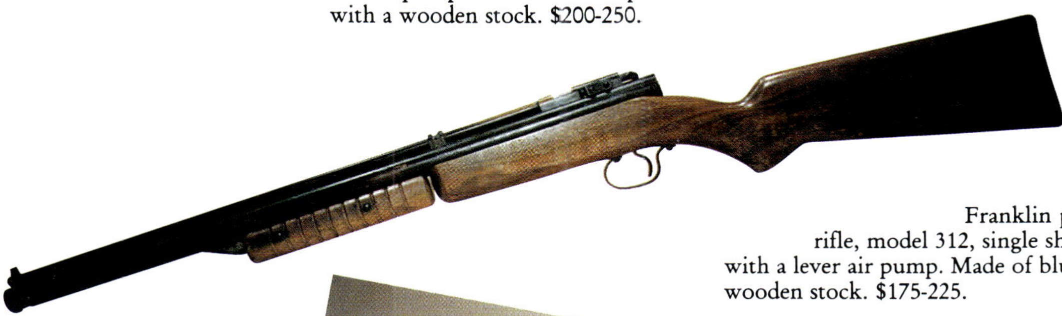

Benjamin Franklin pneumatic air rifle, model 312, single shot .22 Cal. pellet with a lever air pump. Made of blued brass with a wooden stock. $175-225.

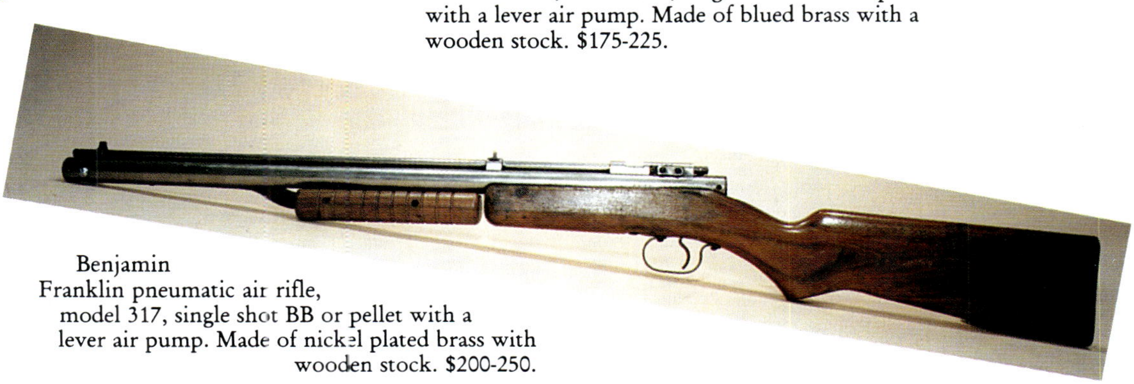

Benjamin Franklin pneumatic air rifle, model 317, single shot BB or pellet with a lever air pump. Made of nickel plated brass with wooden stock. $200-250.

BB Guns—Daisy Parts

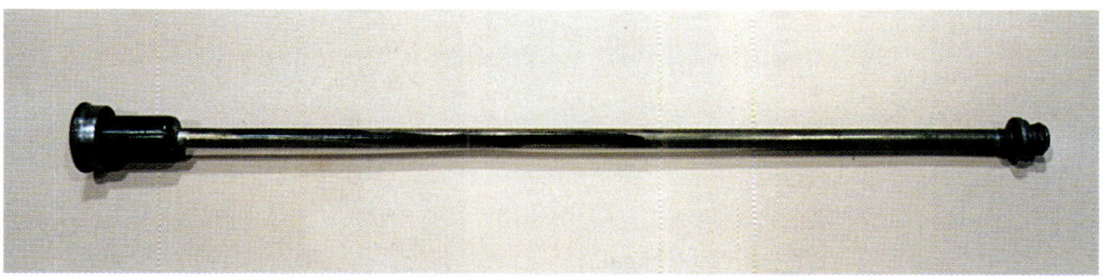

Model 25 Daisy single shot cork tube, first type. You take out the BB shot tube and put in the cork shot tube, put one round cork ball in the end of the pump and shoot. Hard to find. $100-125.

Model 25 Daisy single shot cork tube, second type. You take out the BB shot tube and put in the cork shot tube, put one round of cork in the end, pump and shoot. Hard to find. $75-100.

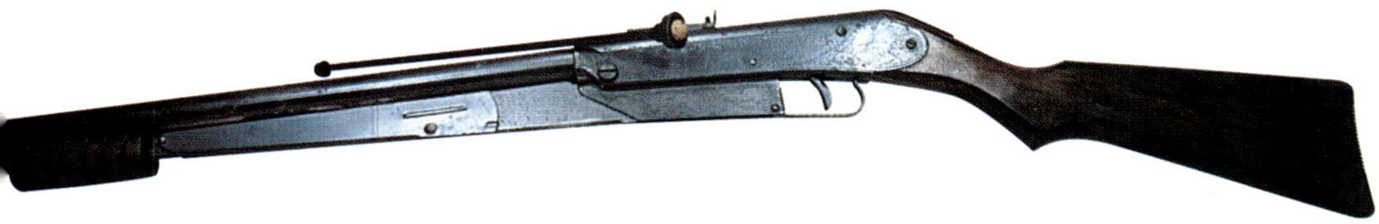

Number 25 Daisy Pump 50 Shot
Force Feed with a cork tube. $200-250.

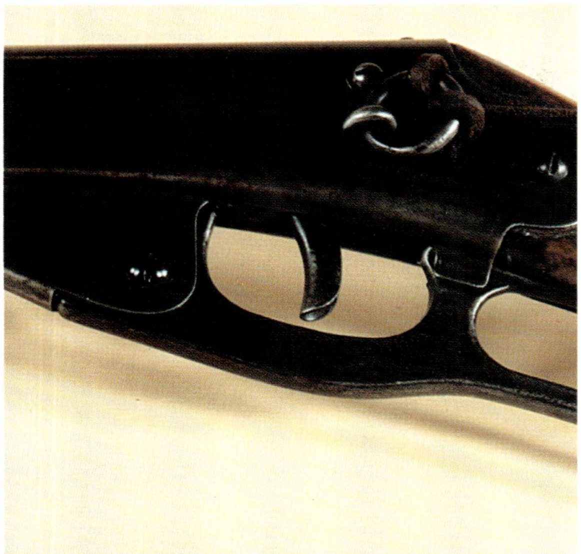

Daisy cast iron lever, made from the late 1800s to 1942. $20-30.

Daisy aluminum lever, made in the 1950s. $5-10.

Daisy aluminum lever, made from 1942 to 1954. $5-10.

Daisy aluminum lever, made in the late 1950s. $5-10.

Number 111 Daisy Red Ryder Carbine Model #40 wooden forearms. The wooden forearm on the bottom is an original—note the longer curve. The example on the top was made in the 1990s.

To tell if the plunger head inside this Red Ryder is ok: Do not cock the gun, unscrew the shot tube, pull it out, and lower it back in. If the tube sticks out of the barrel this much, the plunger head is ok. Cock the gun and screw in the shot tube.

To tell if the plunger head inside this Red Ryder is ok: Do not cock the gun, unscrew the shot tube, pull it out, and lower it back in. If it sticks out of the barrel this much, the plunger head is broken off and the gun will not shoot a BB, but when cocked and shot it will sound like it will. The gun is broken and the value is greatly reduced.

Number 111 Daisy Red Ryder Carbine Model #40 steel band. There is a steel band that goes on the wooden forearm. Note: the steel band on the left is an original, measuring 1/2" wide; the band on the right is 3/8" wide and was made in the 1990s.

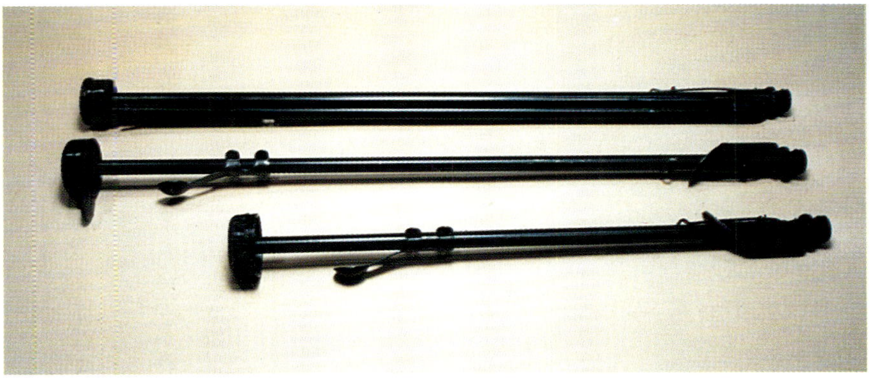

Replacement shot tubes for the Model 25 top, Red Ryder center, and the bottom will fit most of the short, lever models.

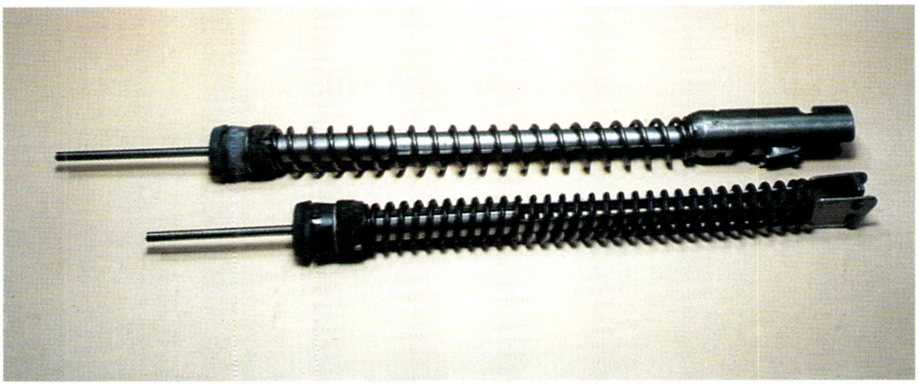

Spring and plunger head assembly. Replacement parts for the Model 25 Daisy Pump and the Number 111 Daisy Red Ryder carbine model #40. The Model 25 is shown on the top and the Red Ryder is on the bottom.

To tell if the plunger head inside this Model 25 is ok: Do not cock the gun, unscrew the shot tube, pull it out, and lower it back in. If it sticks out of the barrel this much, the plunger head is ok. Cock the gun and screw in the shot tube.

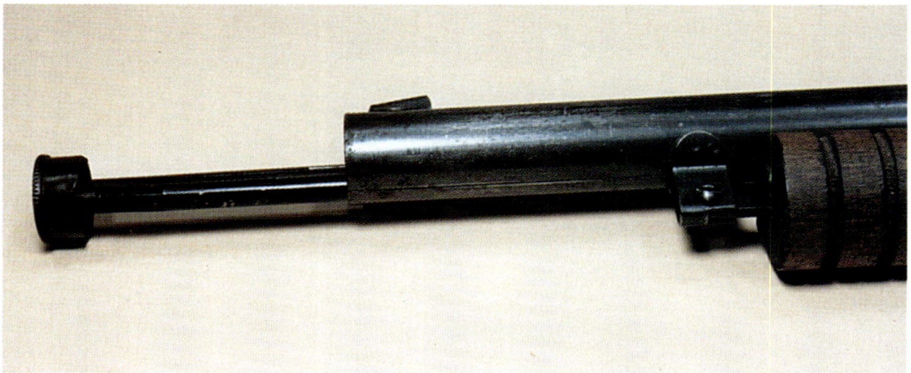

To tell if the plunger head inside this Model 25 is ok: Do not cock the gun, unscrew the shot tube, pull it out, and lower it back in. If the tube sticks out of the barrel this much, the plunger head is broken off and the gun will not shoot a BB; however, when cocked and shot, it may sound like it will. Still, the gun is broken and the value is greatly reduced.

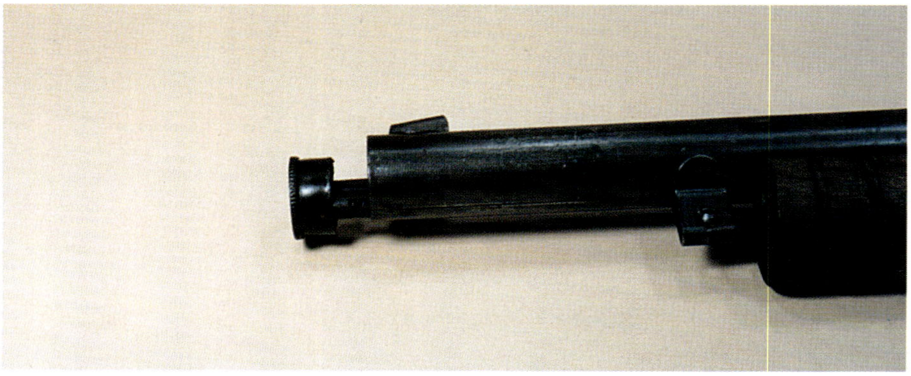

Red Ryder shot tube holding spring. If this spring is missing or broken, the BB will fall out of the barrel when you point the barrel down. The spring holds the BB in until you shoot it.

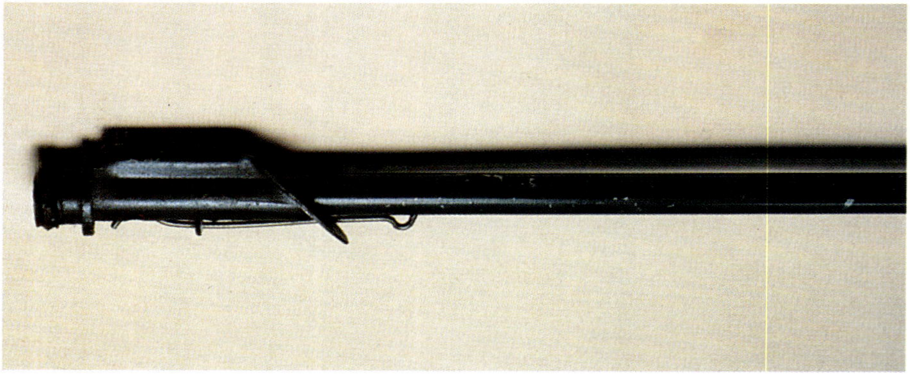

Model 25 shot tube holding spring. If this spring is missing or broken, the BB will fall out of the barrel when you point the barrel down. The spring holds the BB in until you shoot it.

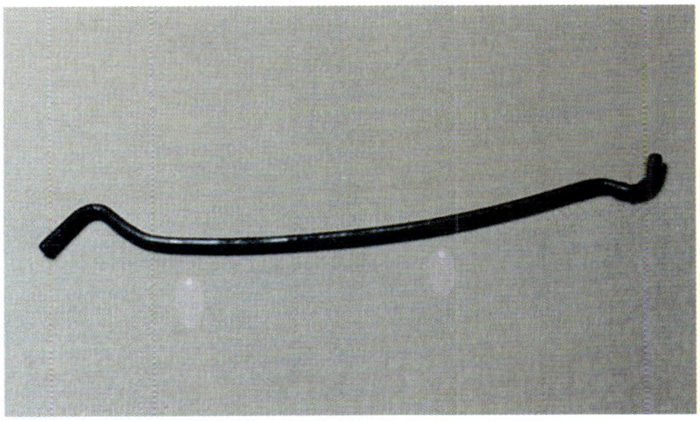

This is the holding spring. It is the same spring for both the Red Ryder and the Model 25.

This is the original screw that holds the Daisy Model 25 together.

Number 111 Daisy Red Ryder Carbine Model #40 inscriptions. The words and horseman on this wooden stock were burned in with an electric iron. The electric iron was used to inscribe the words and image until the early 1950s.

This is the replacement screw made in the 1990s that holds the Daisy Model 25 together.

Number 111 Daisy Red Ryder Carbine Model #40 inscriptions. To cut costs, the words and horseman on this wooden stock were stamped in. Note that there is little depth to the words and horseman as compared to the electric iron.

The CO2 cylinder on the left is the first size used in CO2 guns, measuring 2 1/2" long. It is hard to find. The cylinder on the right is the new type, measuring 3 1/4" long, which you can still buy today. Old type: $2-3 each.

Daisy BBs made in Rogers, Arkansas. $3-5.

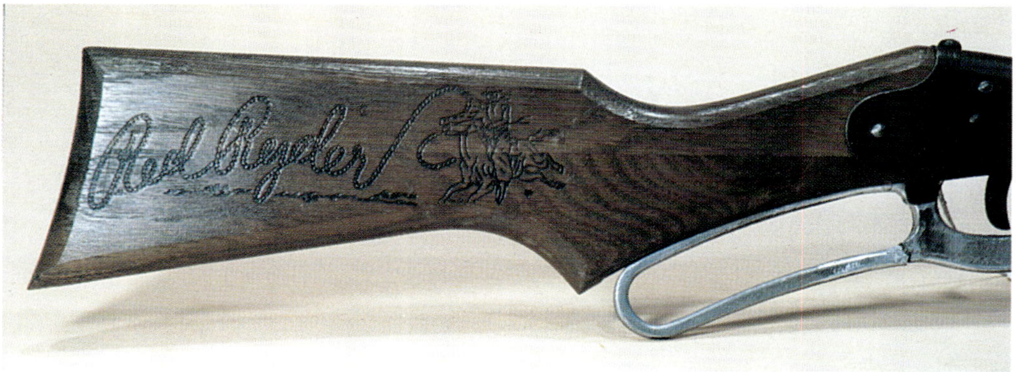

This is a new Red Ryder Carbine Model #40 wooden stock. $5-10.

This is a new wooden stock that will fit most Daisy lever stocks. $5-10.

Daisy BBs made in Plymouth, Michigan. Note: the BBs look the same — look on the back to see where they came from. $15-20.

XL BBs, 1 1/4 oz. Made by the Federal Cartridge Corporation, Minneapolis, Minnesota, in the 1950s. $5-10.

Daisy air rifle target made of paper. Made from the 1950s-1960s. 5" x 4 1/2". $2-3 each.

Daisy Targeteer target made of paper. Made from 1937-1952. 5" x 4 1/2". $3-5 each.

Daisy Targeteer target set with 25 paper targets measuring 5" x 4 1/2", with tin target spinners and BBs. $75-100.

Daisy paper target holder made of steel in Plymouth, Michigan. 5" x 4 3/4". $50-75.

Daisy cleaning kit made in Plymouth, Michigan. Box only: $30-40.

Daisy cleaning kit made in Plymouth, Michigan. Hard to find complete. $100-150.

Christmas advertisement of December 1934. This Daisy advertisement appeared in the Schweinler Press of New York, printed in 1934. Of all the Daisy advertisements that I have seen, this is one of the best. Read along and listen to the salesmanship of 1934: "A Daisy! Number ONE choice on the Christmas lists of millions of red blooded American boys. And no wonder-NOTHING ELSE WILL GIVE YOU the YEAR 'ROUND FUN a Daisy will, whether it's stalking through the woods on a hot summer afternoon like Daniel Boone- back yard shooting contests in spring or fall-or hot competition in your own basement rifle range on those long cold winter nights. Indoors-outdoors-winter or summer, there's no limit to the fun you can have with a Daisy...Of course you want a Daisy for Christmas and we know a swell way for you to go about getting yours. Here's the dope: Send TODAY for our big four color catalogue that shows every one of these fine 1934 Daisys in detail. Study it-pick out your DAISY, (and just to make sure it's the right one go see it and test it at your Daisy dealers) then put a circle around YOUR DAISY in the catalogue, and give the catalogue to Dad or Mother. Tell them, that's YOUR idea of a real Christmas present and that Christmas just won't be Christmas unless you get it. But don't stop there-keep working on Dad and Mother EVERY DAY. If you'll follow this plan that new Daisy's "in the bag". Now go to work and STICK TO IT!! GET THAT DAISY!! This is an original, not a copy! $125-175.

Christmas advertisement of January 1935. This Daisy advertisement appeared in the Schweinler Press of New York, printed in January 1935. In the December advertisement of the Schweinler Press, Daisy told you how to get your Daisy for Christmas. In this ad, they tell you that you can still get your Daisy with the Christmas money Grandma sent you. This is also an original, not a copy. $100-125.

Daisy advertisement on the back of a comic book in the late 1950s. $5-10.

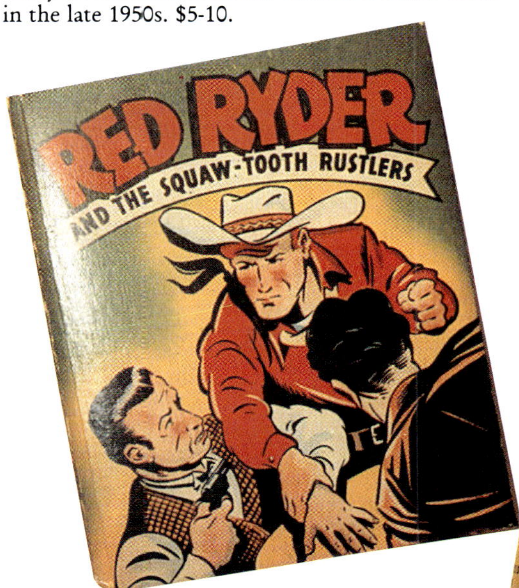

Red Ryder and the Squaw Tooth Rustlers, copyright 1946. 3 1/2" x 4 1/2" 347 pages. The "better little book" Hawley publications. $40-50.

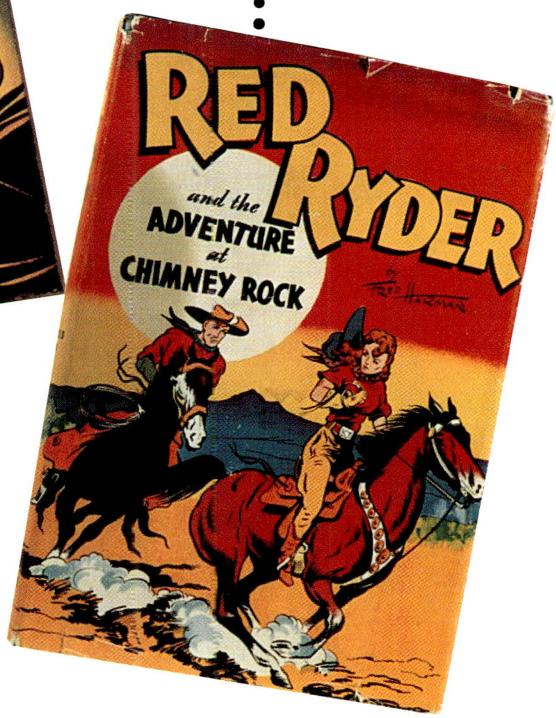

Red Ryder and the Adventure at Chimney Rock. Hard back book, copyright 1946. 5 1/2" x 8". 249 pages. $50-60.

BB Guns—New Daisy Rifles

This Red Ryder with a classic comic book was made in Rogers, Arkansas, in 1989. It was sold for about $35.00. Now it brings $60-80.

Model 1938B Limited Edition "It's a Daisy" Red Ryder. Limited Edition box. $80-100.

Model 1938B Limited Edition "It's a Daisy" Red Ryder. This Limited Edition commemorates the 100th anniversary of the Daisy Manufacturing Co. which changed from the Plymouth Iron Windmill Co. on January 26, 1895. Only 1,938 of these guns were made. $250.

Daisy Power Line 990. Dual-Power CO2 or pump, shoots .177 caliber ammo single shot pellet or 100 shot BB repeater. This has to be one of the most outstanding BB guns ever made. If you are out of pellets, use BBs; if you are out of CO2 cylinders, pump it up. $50-70.

Daisy Power Line 880. Pump, shoots .177 caliber ammo single shot pellets or BBs. Still made today. $40-50.

Daisy Model 880. 20th Anniversary Limited Edition Power Line 880. Pump, shoots .177 caliber pellet or 100 shot BB repeater. Made for one year in 1992. $200-250.

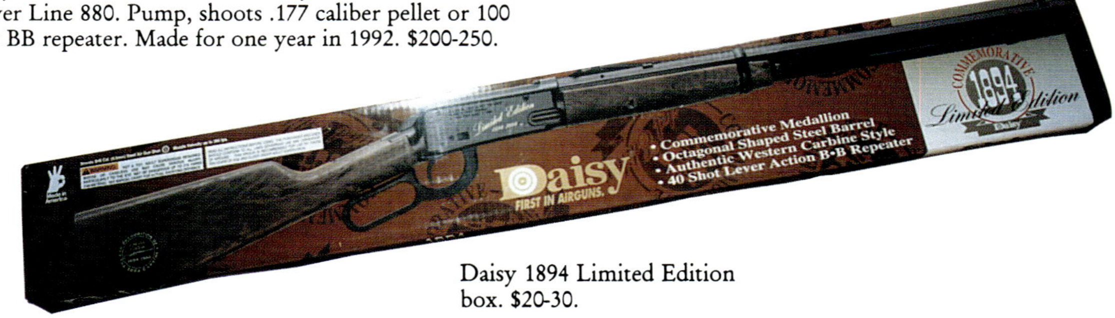

Daisy 1894 Limited Edition box. $20-30.

Daisy 1894 Limited Edition 1894-1994, 40 shot lever action BB repeater. Made in 1994. $60-80.

Daisy Model 970, multi-pump pneumatic. Comes in Model 917, .177 Cal. pellet, or 922, .22 Cal. pellet. Made of steel with a high grade wooden stock. This gun sold for $80 in the early 1990s.

Daisy Eagle with a 4 X scope. Pump, shoots .177 caliber pellet or BBs. Still made today. $30-40.

Daisy 914, single pump pneumatic BB or pellet. Made in the early 1990. $30-40.

Candy Shooters

Astra Shooter candy shooter, 3" long x 2" high x 1/2" wide. Made of plastic in the 1950s. Turn the gun upside down until a candy falls into the barrel and then put the gun barrel in your mouth and pull the trigger. The candy shoots into your mouth. Of all the candy dispensers that I have seen, this one is *unbelievably* bad! It taught kids to put gun barrels in their mouths and pull the triggers to get candy. What were they thinking in the 1950s?! Made in Japan. $30-40.

Candy shooter, 3" long x 2" high x 1/2" wide. Made of plastic in the 1950s. You put the barrel in your mouth and crank the lever on the side. The candy shoots into your mouth. This is another candy dispenser that was teaching kids the wrong thing. I can see why these are not made any more. Hard to find. $20-30.

Hasbro's M&M candy gun. The gun is 4 1/4" long x 3 3/4" high x 1" wide. Made of plastic, the set sold for 88 cents. Note that the bag of M&Ms is missing. You see why these are not made any more: Made for Hasbro by Hassenfeld Bros. Inc., Central Falls, R.1., U.S.A. Price for the gun alone is $150-175. The card with the gun, badge, holster, and original M&M candy is very rare and is valued at $250-300.

Pez candy pop out watch, shoots out candy, 1 1/2" x 1 1/2". Made of plastic in China for Dream Castle the 1980s. $5-10.

Cap Shooters

Sea Serpent, 3 1/2" long. Single shot made of cast iron by Stevens in 1890. Very rare. $700-900.

Unxld, 4 1/2" long. Single shot, made of cast iron in 1880, maker unknown. $150-200.

No Name, 4 1/2" long. Cast iron single shot. Made in 1878. $150- 200.

Favor, 6 1/8" long. Single shot, made of cast iron in 1880 by Stevens. $200-250.

Firecracker gun. Cast iron made by Stevens in 1872. $150-200.

Terror, 4 1/4" long. Single shot, made of cast iron by Dent in 1925. $150-200.

Federal Kilgore No. 1, 5 1/4" long. Automatic, made of cast iron by Kilgore in 1920. $150-200.

Bang-O, 7" long. Automatic, made of cast iron by Stevens in 1938. $150-200.

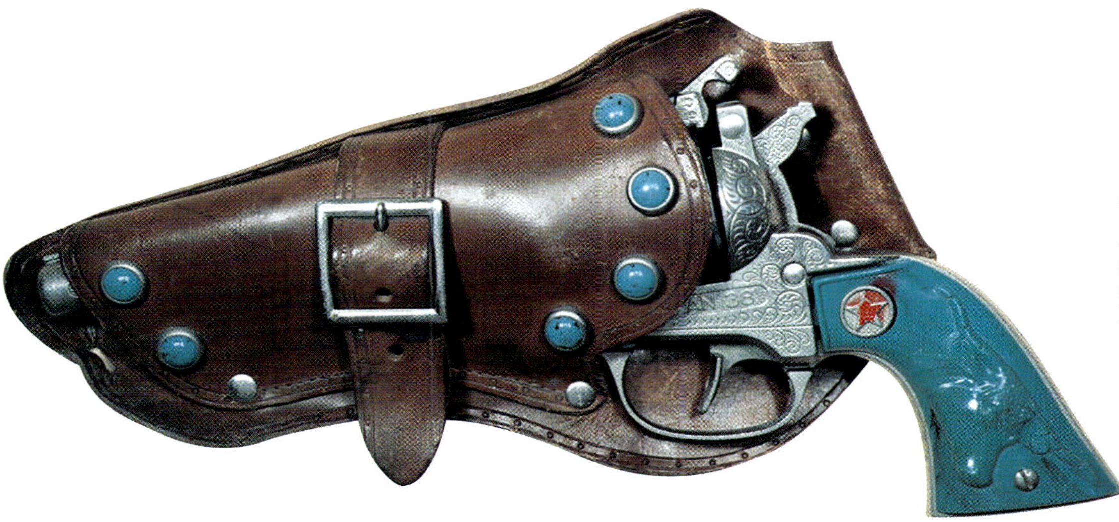

Texan 38, 11 1/4" long. Automatic, made of die-cast metal by Hubley. This is a cowgirl cap gun with a holster. Hard to find. $300-350.

Smoky Joe, 8 1/8" long. Automatic, made of cast iron by Hubley in 1940. Note: this is a new replacement grip, the original is brown. Hard to find. $250-300.

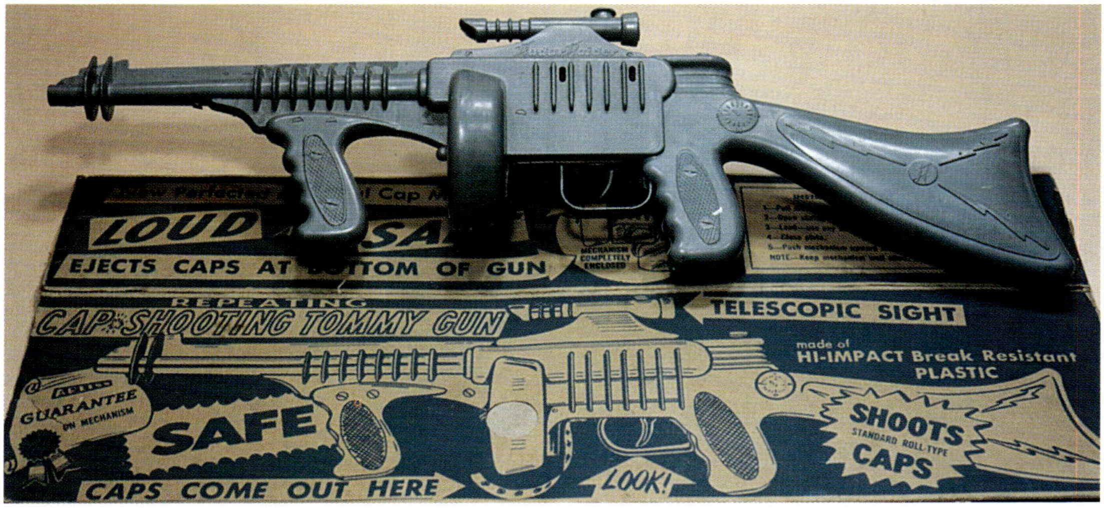

Radar Raider with the original box, 17 3/4" long x 5 1/2" x 1 1/4" wide. Made of plastic by Arliss Co. Inc., Brooklyn 5, New York, in the 1950s. $100-150.

S W Cast Iron Single Shot blank, 6" long. Made by Kenton in 1925. $60-80.

American Bull Dog single shot blank, 4 1/2" long. Made of cast iron by Kenton in 1907. $80-100.

S W Cast Iron Single Shot blank, 4" long. Made by Kenton in 1925. $60-80.

Opposite page:
Rapid Fire Machine Gun, 6" tall x 6 5/8" long. Made of cast iron, shoots rolled caps by cranking the handle. Has "Anti-Aircraft Rapid Fire Machine Gun" printed on the other side. Made by Grey Iron in 1929. Very rare. $800-900.

Cane American Repeater Model 9, 5 7/8" long x 1 1/4" wide x 1/2". Shoots a roll of caps. Made of steel, maker unknown. Patented 11/1/1904. $200-300.

Cap cannon, nickel plated cast iron single shot, on a wood base with original caps. Shoots BBs. $125-150.

Cane, 2 1/2" long. Made of steel, shoots a wad of caps that is folded together. Made around 1900, maker unknown. $150-200.

Jolly Roger pirate cannon in the original package, 4 3/4" x 2 1/4" x 1 3/8". Made of pot metal by the Callen Mfg. Corp. $80-100.

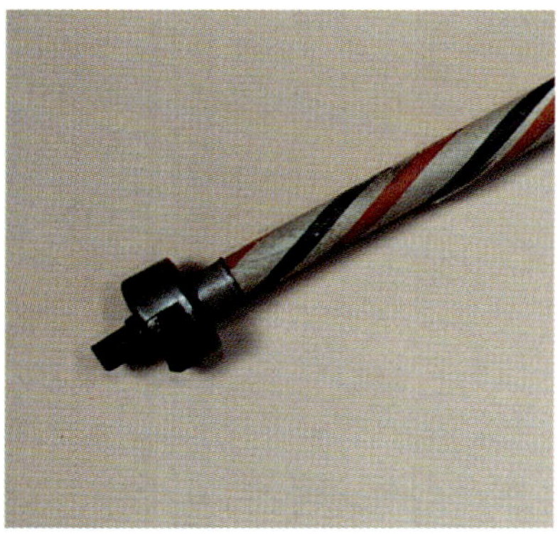

Universal Fireworks Co., 25" long. The tip is made of steel with a paper covered wooden handle. Patent # 2208389. Made in 1940. $50-75.

Cane, 26" long. The tip is made of steel and nylon with a painted wooded handle. Made in the 1950s, maker unknown. $20-30.

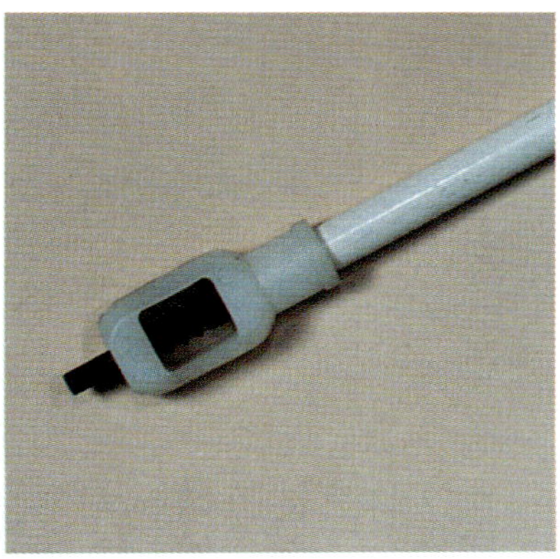

Cap bomb, single shot. Made of cast iron by Ives in 1890. Hard to find. $150-200.

Single shot blank gun, shoots blanks or a single # 9 lead shot, 1 1/4" long. Made in Japan in the 1950s. $100-125.

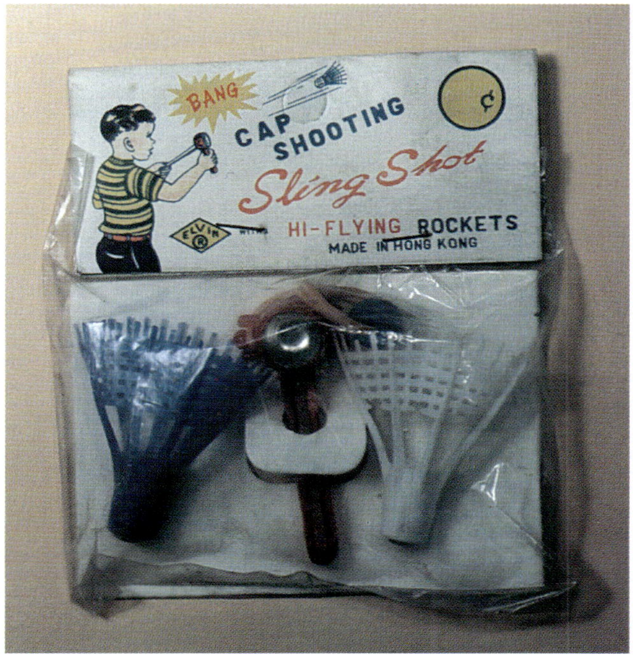

Sling shot rockets, 1 3/4" long. Made in Hong Kong in the 1960s. $10-15.

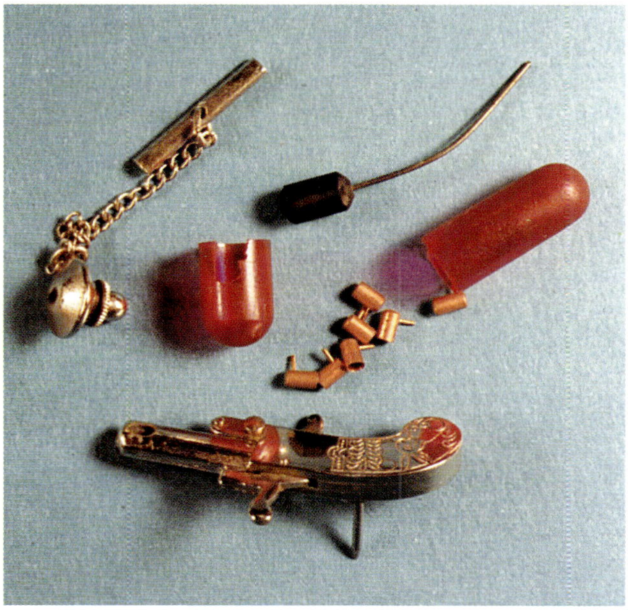

Single shot tie tack blank gun, shoots blanks only, 1 1/4" long. Made in Japan in the 1950s. $75-100.

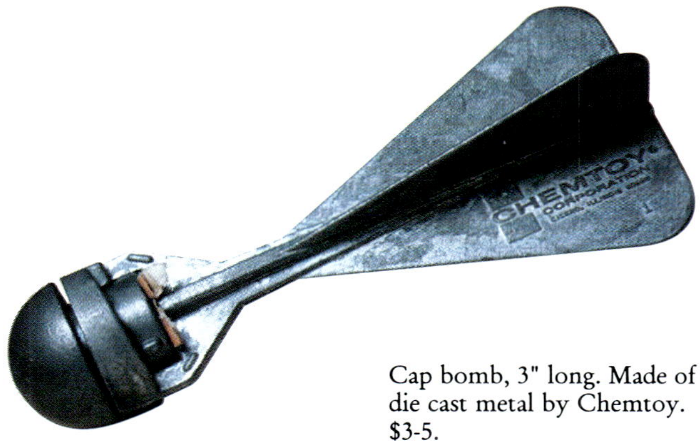

Cap bomb, 3" long. Made of die cast metal by Chemtoy. $3-5.

Rocket cap bomb, 5" tall. Made of plastic in Hong Kong in the 1970s. $5-10.

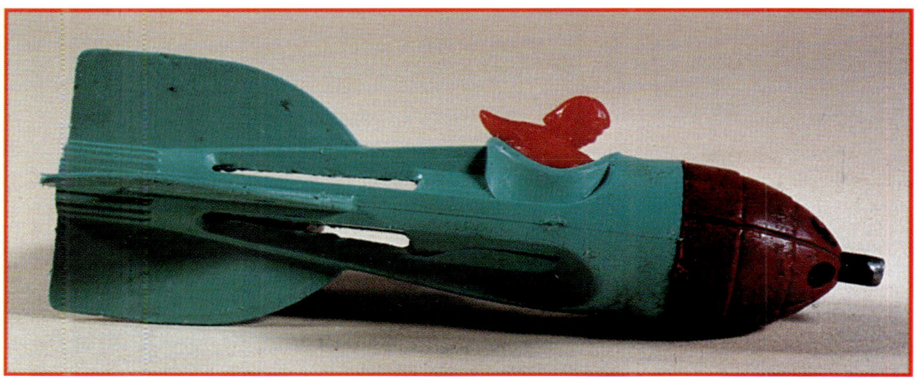

Sky Jet rocket cap bomb, 3 1/2" long. Made of plastic by Ashley Mfg. Co., N.Y.C. Model E, made in the 1960s. $15-20.

Sky Jet rocket cap bomb, 3 1/2" long. Made of plastic by Ashley Mfg. Co., N.Y.C. Model D, made in the 1960s. $15-20.

Rocket cap bomb, 3 1/2" long. Made of plastic in Hong Kong in the 1960s. $5-10.

Rocket cap bomb, 3 1/2" long. Made of plastic by the Royal Tot Mfg. Co., 200 Fifth Ave., N.Y.C., in the 1950s. $15-20.

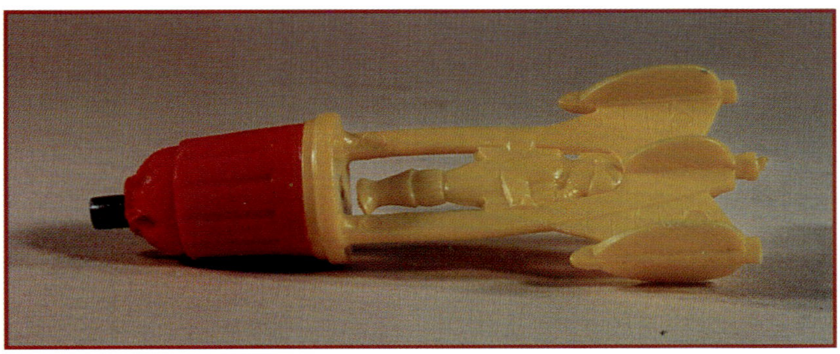

Rocket cap bomb, 3 1/2" long. Made of plastic in the 1960s. $5-10.

Rocket cap grenade, 2 1/2" long. Made of plastic by Arkin A-OK Products Co., Novi, Michigan 48050, in the 1980s. $5-10.

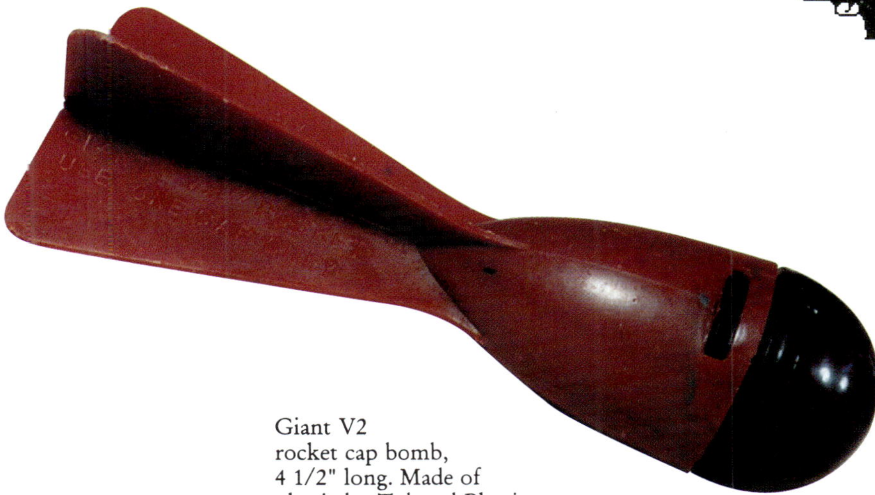

Giant V2 rocket cap bomb, 4 1/2" long. Made of plastic by Tybond Plastics, Chicago, Illinois, in the 1950s. $30-40.

Cap grenade, 3" long. Made of die cast metal by Callen Mfg.Corp., Matwood, Illinois, in the 1970s. $5-10.

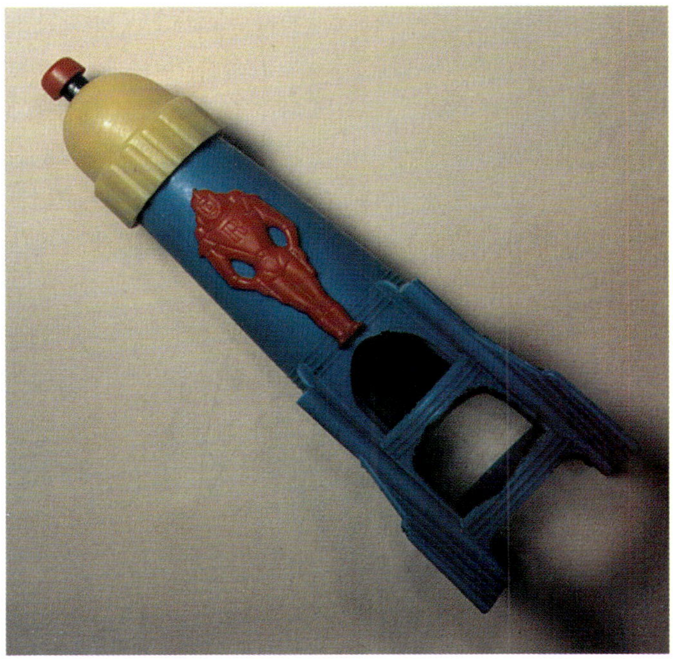

Rocket cap bomb, 5 3/4" long. Made of plastic in the 1960s. $20-30.

V2 rocket cap bomb, 3 1/4" long. Made of plastic by Tybond Plastics, Chicago, Illinois, in the 1950s. $15-20.

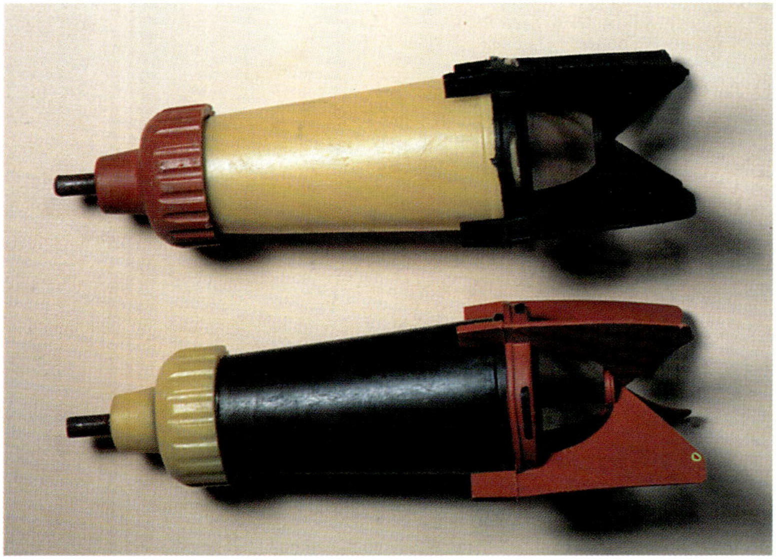

Rocket cap bomb, 5 1/4" long. Made of plastic in the 1960s. $15-20.

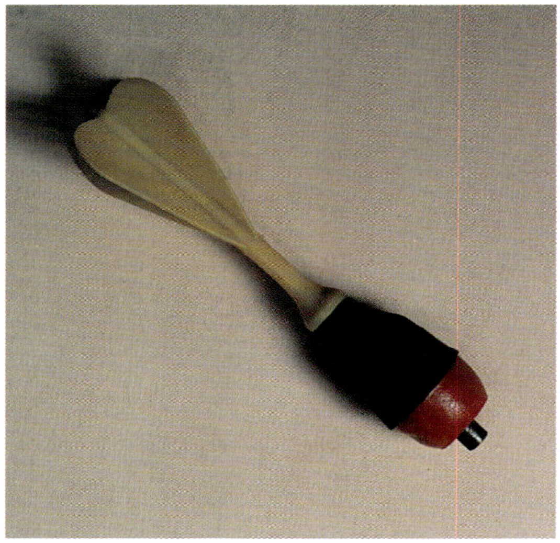

Rocket cap bomb, 3 5/8" long. Made of plastic by Palmer Plastics Inc., Woodside, New York, in the 1960s. $5-10.

Three stage rocket cap bomb, 9" long. Made of plastic in the 1960s. $20-30.

Rocket cap bomb, 3 3/8" long. Made of plastic. $5-10.

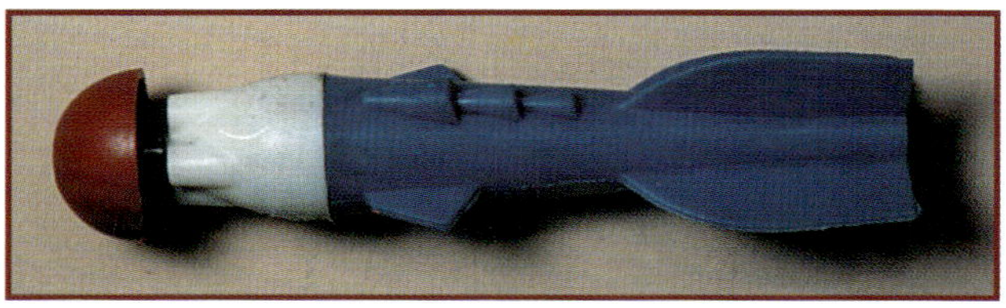

Rocket cap bomb, 3 7/8" long. Made of plastic. $5-10.

Liberty cap bomb, 5 1/4" tall. Made of plastic in Hong Kong in the 1960s. $15-20.

Dive Bomber with cap bomb with the original package. Made of pot metal by the Callen Mfg. Corp. in the 1960s. $75-100.

Triple shot cap bomb, 2 3/4" tall. Made of plastic in Hong Kong in the 1960s. $10-15.

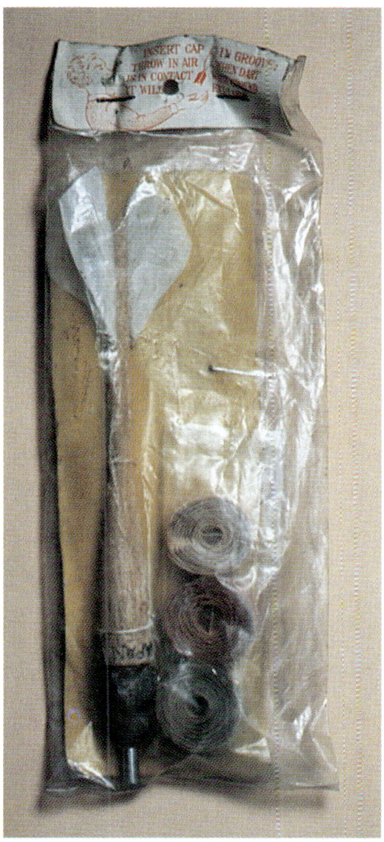

Cap Grenade with the original package. Made of pot metal by the Callen Mfg. Corp. in the 1960s. $40-50.

Cap dart, 5 1/4" long. Made of wood and metal in Japan in the 1950s. Hard to find. $30-40.

Dart Cap Bomb Game with the original box. Made of tin with plastic rocket darts by the Royal Tot Mfg. Co., 200 Fifth Ave., N.Y.C., in the 1950s. $80-100.

Cap Shooting Tank, 5 7/8" long x 3" high x 3 3/4" wide. Made of tin in Japan in the 1950s and 1960s. Note: the top of the turret is missing on this tank. The price for a complete tank is $150-200.

Cap Grenade, 4 1/2" tall. Made of plastic. $10-15.

Cap shooting pad and pen with an original box. When you take out the pen, a cap will go off. Made in the 1950s. $50-75.

Cap Grenade, 4 1/2" tall. Made of plastic. $10-15.

Cap shooting cigarette case. Patent # 2640297. Made of plastic by Adams in the 1950s. $30-40.

Thief-Proof Lock, cap lock shooter with the original box. When installed on a door, and someone tries to open the door, a very loud cap goes off and the chain will keep the door closed. Made by the Universal Safety Lock Co., Detroit, Michigan, in 1928. Rare. $150-200.

Above left:
Cork pistol, 11" long x 3 1/4" high x 3/4" wide. Made of wood and tin beer cans. To work, pull the lever back, put the cork in the barrel, and pull the trigger. After World War II, the Japanese made cheap toys from used American beer cans. Some were made as prizes for carnivals in the 1950s. If you look inside of these cork guns, you can still see the original label. This is a Blatz beer can. Hard to find. $40-60.

Center right:
Cork pistol, 11" long x 3 1/4" high x 3/4" wide. Made of wood and tin beer cans. To work, pull the lever back, put the cork in the barrel, and pull the trigger. Once again, after World War II, the Japanese made cheap toys made from used American beer cans; some were made as prizes for carnivals in the 1950s. If you look inside of these cork guns, you can still see the original label. This is a Miller beer can. Hard to find. $40-60.

Cannon cork shooter, with a crank at the back of the gun to shoot a cork, 9 1/2" long. It has three wooden legs. Made by All Metal Products Co., Wyandotte, Michigan, in the 1930s-1940s. $125-150.

Cork Shooting Submachine Gun with the original box, 20" long x 7" high x 2" wide. Made of plastic by Marx Toys in the 1950s. $200 to $300.

Cork Shooting Submachine Gun box.

Daisy Cork Ball Gun, # 68, 28 1/2" long x 1 3/4" high x 1/2" wide. Shoots round cork balls. Made of steel with a wooden stock by the Daisy MFG. Co., Plymouth, Michigan, in the 1950s. $150 to $200.

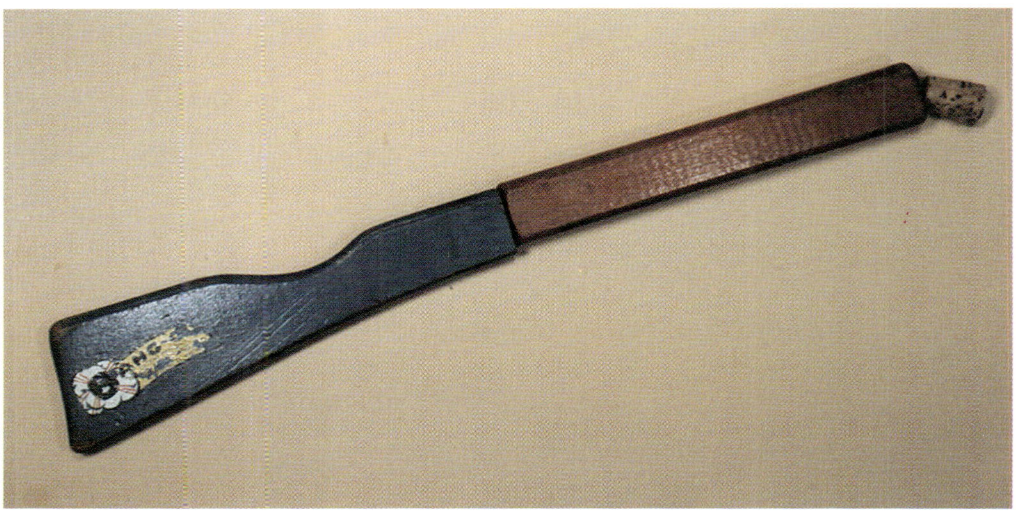

Bang-O Rifle Cork Shooter, 14 3/4" long x 3/4" wide x 2" tall. Made of wood late in World War II by the Air Arms MFG. Co., Cadillac, Michigan. The original price was 89 cents. $30-40.

Bang-O Pistol, Double Barrel, 10 1/2" long x 1 3/4" wide x 3 1/2" tall. Shoots two corks at the same time. Made of wood late in World War II. $30-40.

Cork pistol, 6 1/4" long x 4" high x 1" wide. Made of plastic by Wyandotte Toys in the 1950s and 1960s. $40 to $50.

Cork pistol, 9" long x 3 1/2" high x 1/2" wide. Patent # 1660582. Made of steel by the All Metal Products Co., Wyandotte, Michigan, U.S.A., in the 1920s. $60-80.

Cork pistol, 5 1/2" long x 3 1/2" high x 5/8" wide. Made of steel by an unknown manufacturer, probably in the 1930s. $30-$40.

Cork Ball Cannon, 14" long. Patent # 2493429. Made of tin with 3" rubber tiers in the 1940s. $125-150.

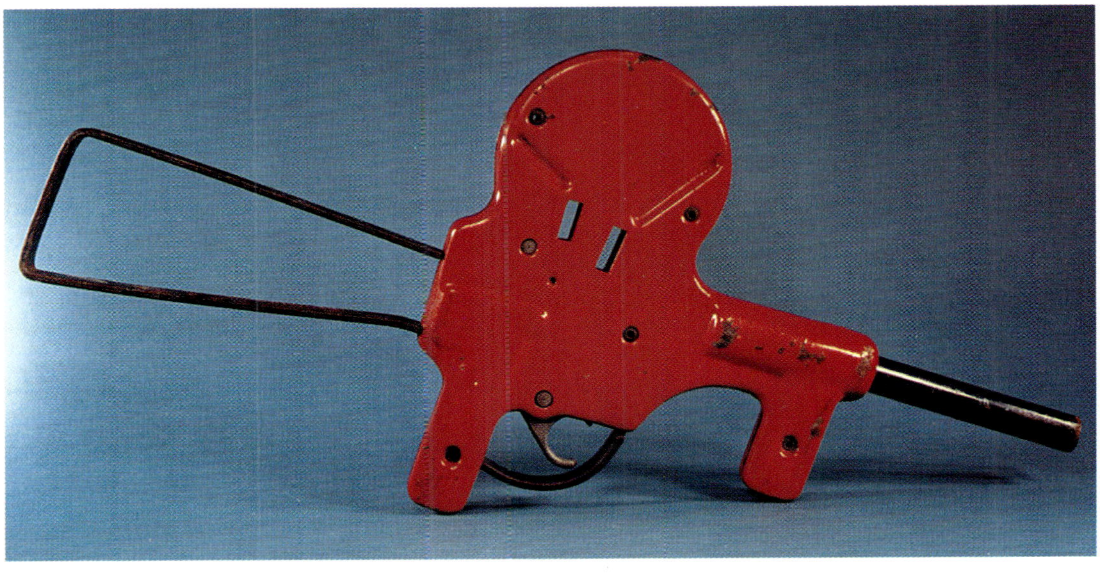

Cork Ball Gun, 17 1/2" long x 8 1/2" high x 1" wide. Made of steel. To work, put small round cork balls in the top and just pull the trigger. This is one of the very few toys of that time that was banned because of injuries to children. Kids used to put marbles in it instead of corks. The marbles would sometimes break, and the gun would then throw out pieces of broken glass. Made in 1930. Very hard to find. $300 to $350.

Pop the Bird Target Game, original box.

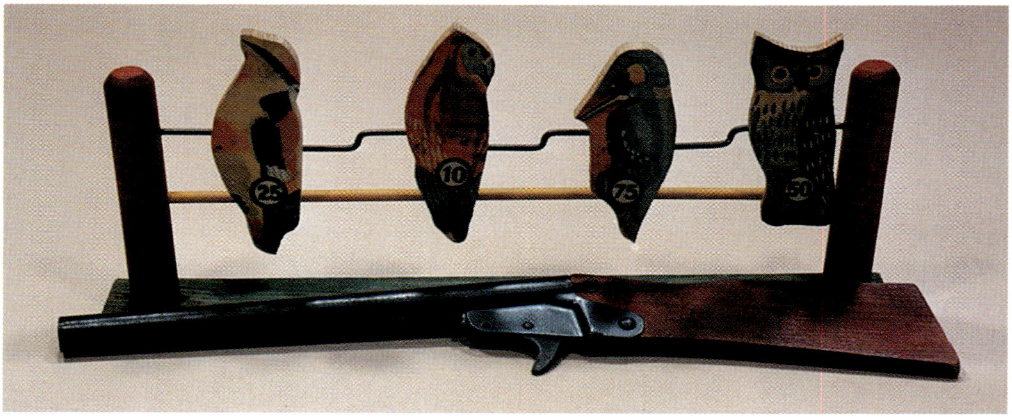

Pop The Bird Target Game in the original box, 13 1/2" long x 1 1/2" high x 1/2" wide. Gun Patent # 1830291. The gun is made of steel and wood. It shoots one cork at a time. The target is 12 1/2" long x 5" high x 1 3/8" wide and is made of wood. The target was made by N.N. Hill Brass Co., East Hampton, Connecticut. The gun was made by the Daisy MFG. Co., Plymouth, Michigan, U.S.A., in the 1930s. $200-300. *Courtesy of Bob and Connie MacKinnon.*

Mobile gun, cork ball shooter, 15" long. Made of tin and wood by Bel-Mar Products Corp, Indianapolis, Indiana, U.S.A. $125-150.

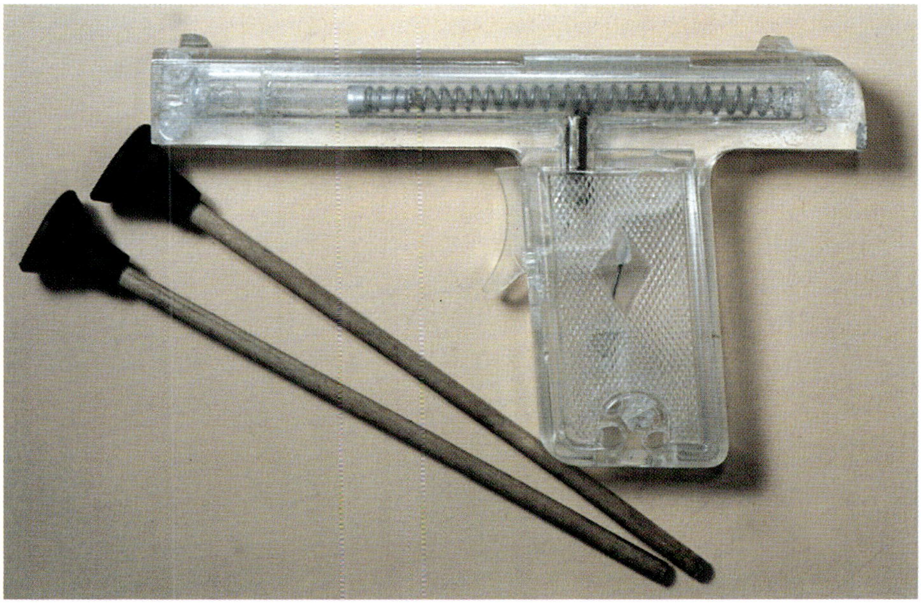

Whizz-z-z Dart pistol, 6" long. Shoots wooden carts with rubber tips. Made of clear plastic by Hinbro Product, Chicago, Illinois. $30-40.

Whizz-z-z dart pistol with the original box, 6" long. Shoots wooden darts with rubber tips. Made in plastic by Hinbro Product, Chicago, Illinois, in the 1950s. $40-60.

Target Practice dart gun with target. The gun measures 5" long; the target measures 7 1/2" x 6 1/2". Made in the 1930s and 1940s. $60-80.

Wyandotte dart shooting pistol with the original box, single shot, 8" long. Made of tin in Wyandotte, Michigan, in the 1940s and 1950s. $125-150.

Dart shooter, no name, 8" long. Made of tin. $10-20.

Wyandotte dart shooter with original box, 6 1/2" long. Made of plastic in Wyandotte, Michigan, in the 1950s. $125-150.

Dart shooter, 6 3/4" long. Made of plastic by Ohio Art, Bryan, Ohio. $10-15.

Dart gun, 6 1/2" long. Made of plastic by Knickerbocker Plastic Co., Glendale, California, in the 1950s. $10-15.

Candid Camera Shot, dart shooter. The target is 9" x 9" and is made of masonite. The camera is made of tin. This shooter was made by Lindstrom Tool and Toy Co., Inc., Bridgeport, Connecticut, in the 1950s. Rare. $200-250.

Whirli Bird target and gun set, original box.

Whirli Bird target and gun set with the original box: contains 1 gun, 1 target, and 2 rubber tipped darts. The gun measures 6 3/4" long. It is made of plastic; the target is made of tin and measures 13 1/2" long x 5 3/4" high. Made by Ohio Art, Bryan, Ohio. $150-200.

Safety dart pistol with the original bag, 3" long. Made of plastic by Pal Plastic, New York 51, in the 1950s. $20-30.

Rangerfinder target dart rifle original box.

Rangerfinder target dart rifle with the original box, 21 3/4" long. Made of steel by All Metal Products Co., Wyandotte, Michigan, in the 1950s. $150-200.

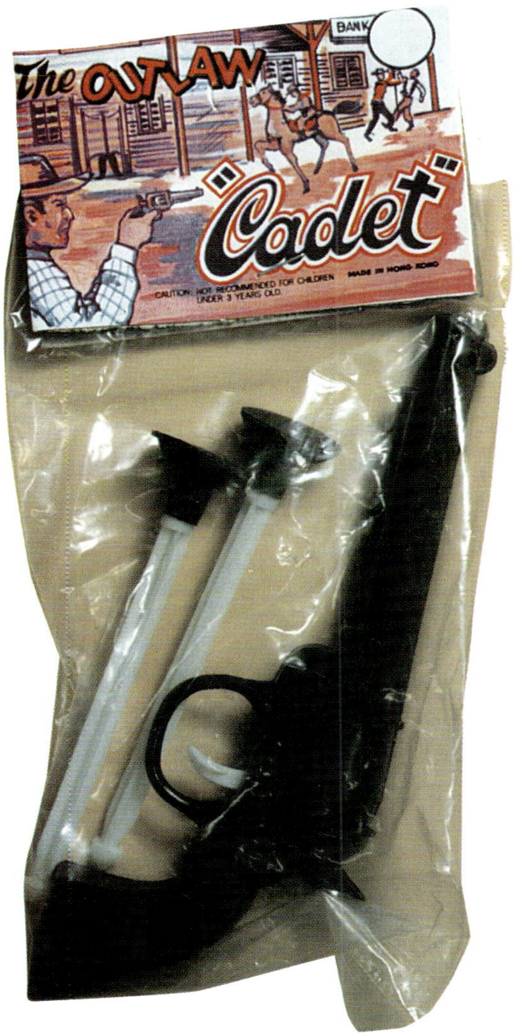

The Outlaw Cadet dart pistol, 5 1/4" long. Made of plastic in Hong Kong in the 1960s. $15-20.

Shooting Game, dart gun, 5 1/4" long. Made of steel in Japan for SSS toy in the 1950s. $15-20.

Marble Shooters

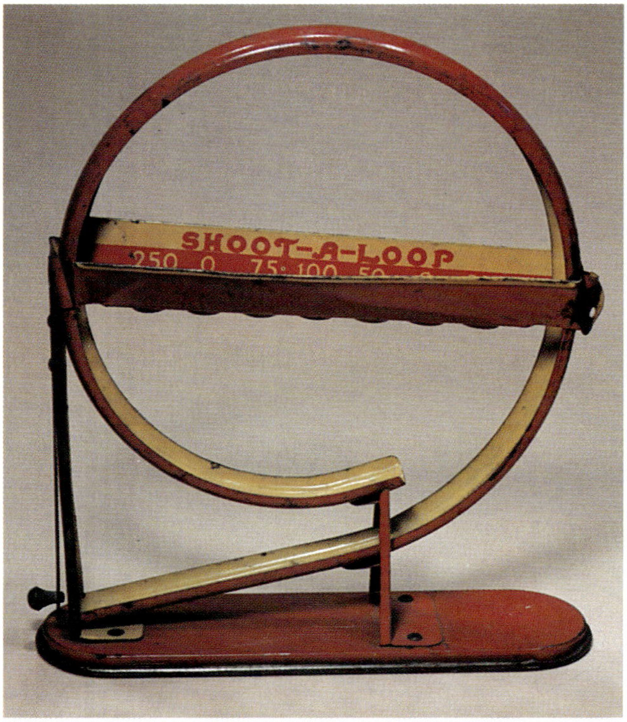

Marble Bingo, 6" high x 16" long. Made of tin by the Wolverine Supply Co., Pittsburgh, Pennsylvania, in the 1950s. $100-125.

Shoot-a-loop, marble shooter, 9" high x 7 1/2" long. Made by the Wolverine Supply Co., Pittsburgh, Pennsylvania, in the 1950s. $100-125.

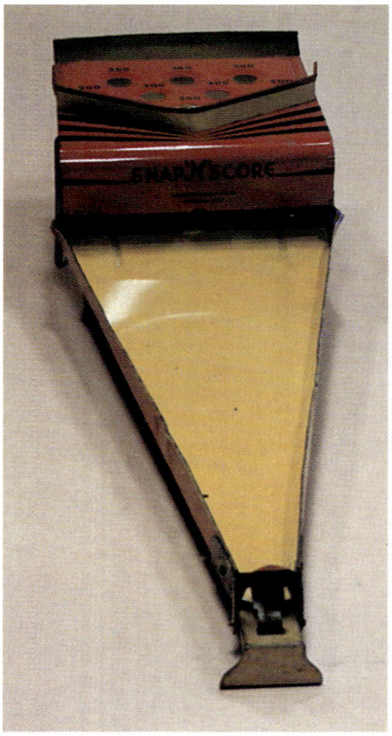

Snap N Score, 5" high x 22" long. Made by the Wolverine Supply Co., Pittsburgh, Pennsylvania, in the 1950s. $100-125.

Marble shooting cannon, 12" long x 4 1/2" high, with a 9 1/4" base. To work, pull the lever under the barrel back, put a marble in muzzle of the barrel, aim by using the two cranks at the back of the cannon, and push the button down at the back of the barrel. Made of steel by B & B Mfg. Co. $150-200.

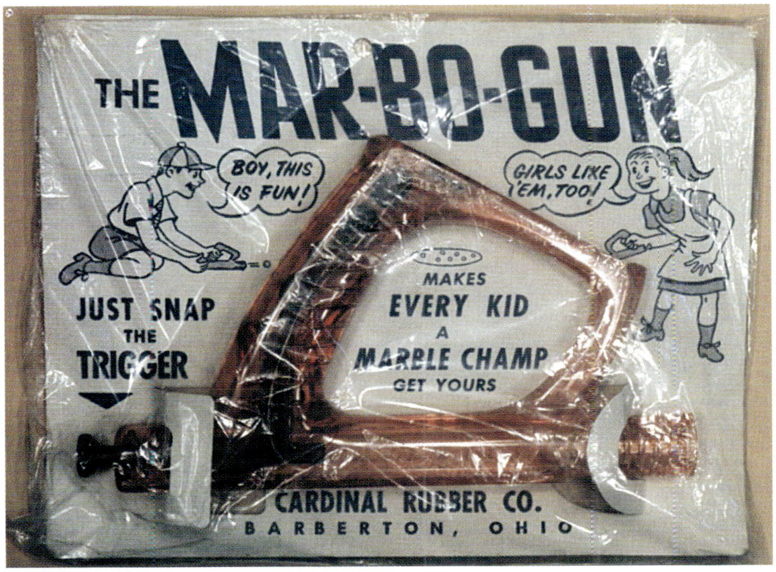

Mar-Bo-Gun with the original package, 8" long x 4 3/4" high. Made of plastic by Cardinal Rubber Co., Barberton, Ohio, in the 1960s. $50-60.

Marble shooter made of wood and steel, 3" long. $5-10.

Marble shooter made of wood and steel, 2" round. $5-10.

Marble shooter made of wood and steel, 4" long. $5-10.

Ping Pong Shooters

K-POP ping pong shooter in the original package. Made by Kusan Inc., Nashville, Tennessee 37212, in the 1960s. $40-50.

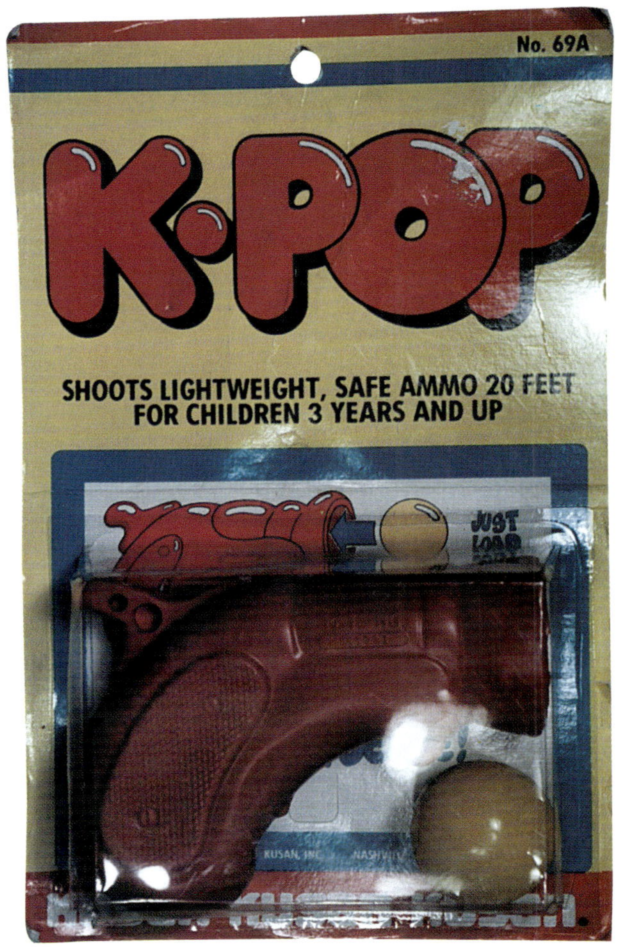

K-POP ping pong shooter, 4 3/4" long. Patent # 2853991. Made of vinyl in the 1960s. $15-20.

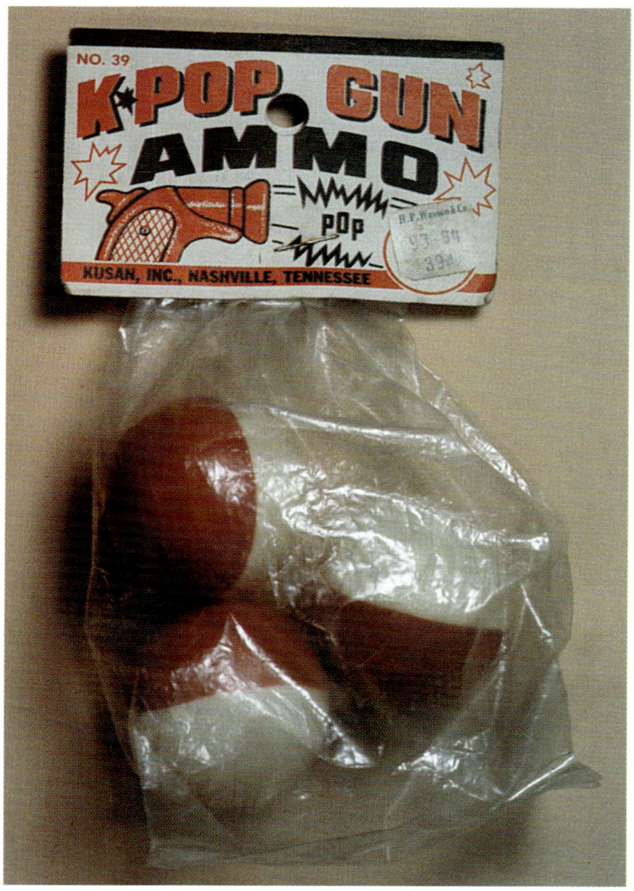

K-POP ping pong ammo in its original package. Made by Kusan Inc., Nashville, Tennessee 37212, in the 1960s. $15-20.

K-POP Repeater ping pong shooter. Made by Kusan Inc., Nashville, Tennessee 37212, in the 1960s. $30-40.

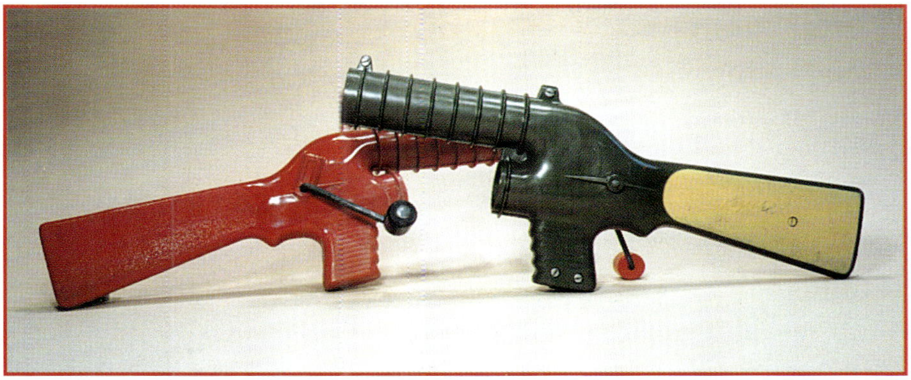

Kazooka, ping pong shooter, 17" x 6 1/2" x 2 1/4". To work, put six ping pong balls in the top end of the long barrel, crank the handle, and the balls come out of the lower barrel. Made of plastic by Kusan in the 1960s. $80-100.

Ball Gun ping pong shooter, 3" long. Made of vinyl in Hong Kong in the 1960s. $15-20.

Ping pong shooter, 10 1/2" long. Made of steel in the 1930s. $80-100.

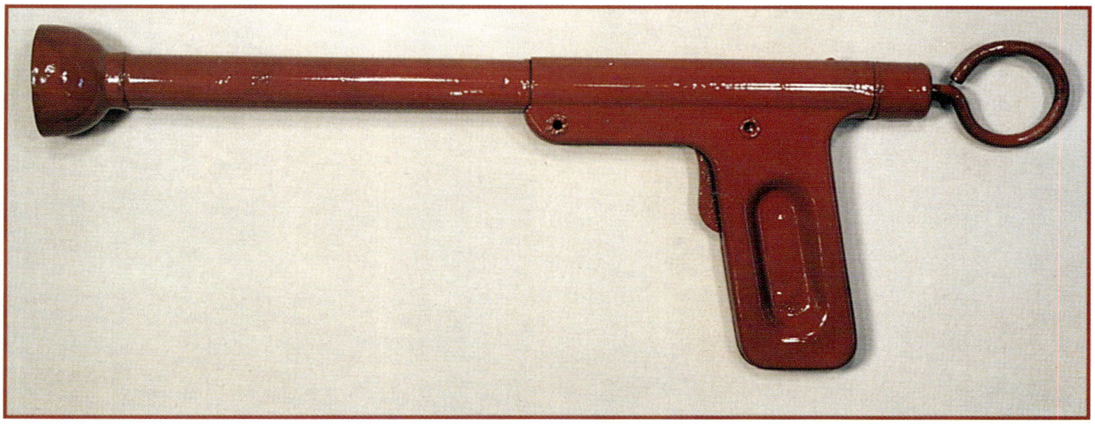

Ping pong shooter, 13 1/2" long. Made of steel in the 1930s. $80-100.

Newell ping pong shooter, shoots one ball at a time, 25" long. Made of plastic and aluminum by Newell Mfg. Co., Lowell, Michigan. $50-75.

Key Chain Puzzles

Jeep, six colors with six pieces, 1 1/2" long. Made in the 1950s. $20-30.

Car, five colors with five pieces, 1 1/2" long. Made in the 1960s. $10-15.

Race Car, five colors with six pieces, 1 5/8" long. Made by Lional in the U.S.A. in the 1950s. $30-$40.

Car, three colors with five pieces, 1 1/2" long. Made in the 1960s. $8-10.

Race Car, five colors with six pieces, 1 5/8" long. Made for Lional in Hong Kong the 1960s. $10-15.

Fire truck, six colors with seven pieces, 2 1/2" long. Made by Lional in the U.S.A. in the 1950s. $30-$40.

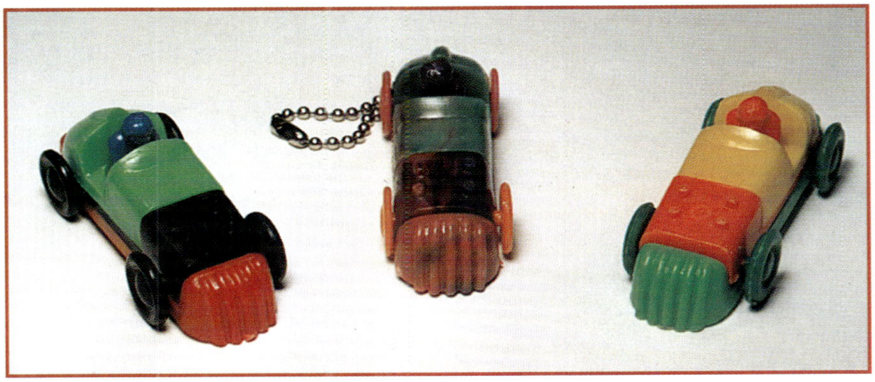

Race Car, five colors with six pieces, 1 5/8" long. Made in Hong Kong in the 1970s. $5-10.

Motor cycle cop, six colors with six pieces, 2 1/2" long. Made in the U.S.A. in the 1950s. Hard to find. $50-$60.

Fire truck, five colors with seven pieces, 2 1/2" long. Made by Lional in the U.S.A. in the 1950s. $25-$35.

Fire truck with original packing and instructions, four colors with seven pieces, 2 1/2" long. Note that the front fireman is missing. Made by Lional in the U.S.A. in the 1950s. $25-$35.

Truck, three colors with six pieces, 1 7/8" long. Made in China in the 1990s. $1-2.

Boat, six colors with six pieces, 2" long. Made of vinyl in the 1980s. $2-3.

Ship, four colors with six pieces, 2 1/4" long. Made in Hong Kong by Fleetwood Toys Inc., NCY 10010, in the 1970s. $3-5.

Airplane, Curtis 2, three colors with six pieces, 1 1/2" long. Made of vinyl in West Germany in the 1970s. $15-20.

Sail Boat, six colors with six pieces, 1 1/2" tall. Made of vinyl in Hong Kong for Dan Brechner & Co., New York, New York 10010, in the 1980s. $2-3.

Airplane, Piper 1, three colors with six pieces, 1 3/4" long. Made of vinyl in West Germany in the 1970s. $15-20.

Rocket, six colors with six pieces, 2 1/4" tall. Made in the 1950s. $30-40.

Airplane, five colors with nine pieces, 2 1/4" long. Made in Hong Kong by Fleetwood Toys Inc., NCY 10010, in the 1970s. $10-15.

Airplane, Jet 1148, six colors with six pieces, 1 1/2" long. Made in the U.S.A. in the 1950s. $30-40.

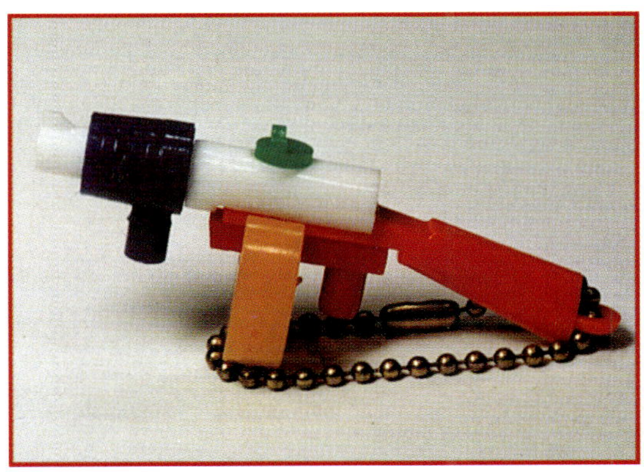

Machine gun, six colors with six pieces, 2 1/2" long. Made in the U.S.A. in the 1950s. Hard to find. $50-60.

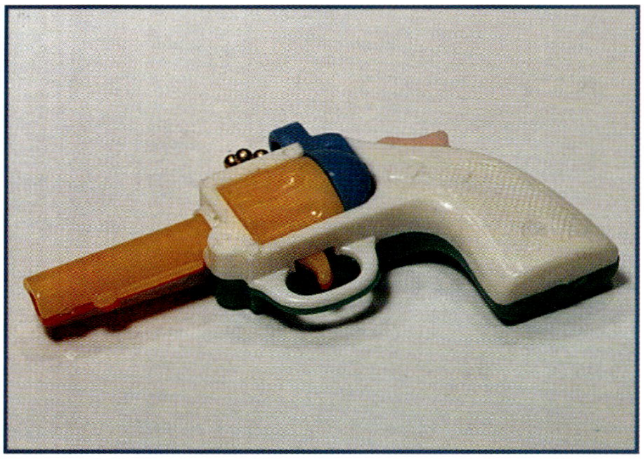

Gun, six colors with six pieces, 2 1/2" long. Made in the 1960s. $25-35.

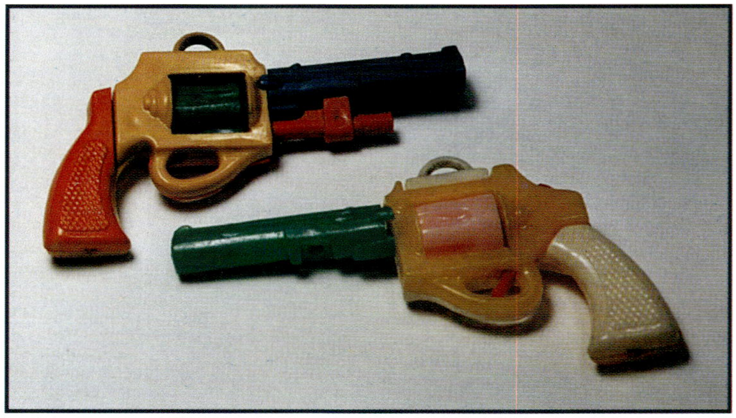

Gun, five colors with five pieces, 2 1/2" long. Made in the 1950s. $30-40.

Gun, four colors with six pieces, 2 1/2" long. Made in the 1960s. $20-30.

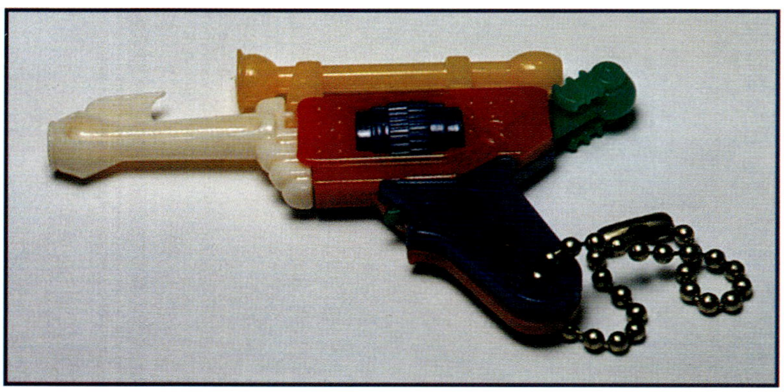

Space Ray Gun, five colors with six pieces, 2 1/2" long. Made in the 1950s. $50-60.

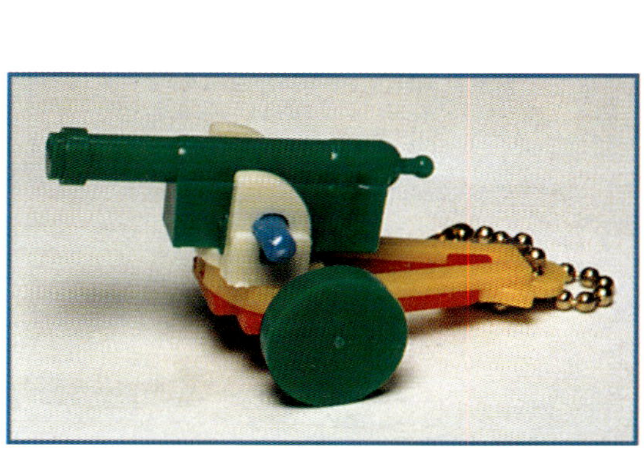

Cannon, five colors with six pieces, 2 1/2" long. Made in the 1970s. $15-20.

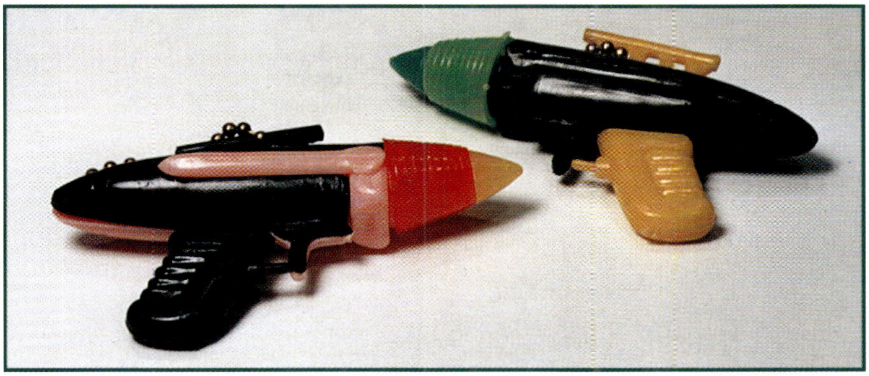

Sace Ray Gun, four colors with six pieces, 2 3/4" long. Made in Hong Kong by Fleetwood Toys Inc., NCY 10010, in the 1970s. $5-10.

Cannon, five colors with six pieces, 2 1/2" long. Made in the 1970s. $15-20.

Heart, six colors with six pieces, 1" tall. Made in the 1950s. $35-45.

Howdy Doody, five colors with five pieces, 2 1/2" tall. Made in the 1950s. $45-55.

Baseball player, five colors with five pieces, 2 1/2" tall. Made in the 1950s-1960s. $20-35.

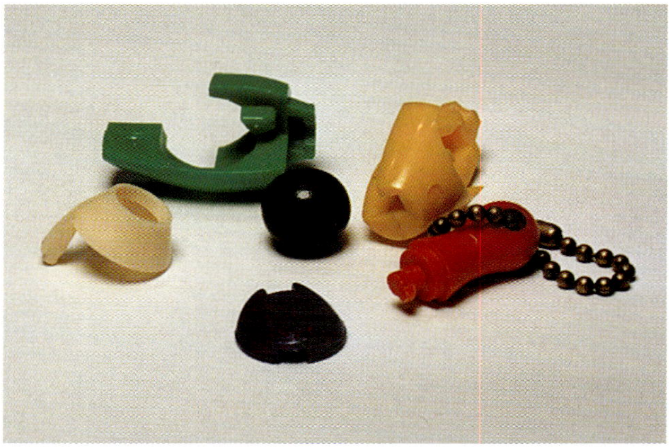

Above left: Wrestler, five colors with six pieces, 1 1/2" tall. Made in the 1950s. Very hard to find. $100-125.

Above right: Ball, earliest type with chain, six colors with six pieces, 3/4" round. Patent # 2178190. Made in the 1940s. Very hard to find. $90-100.

Center left: Ball, second type with cord, six colors with six pieces, 3/4" round. Made in the 1950s. Hard to find. $70-80.

Center right: Ball, either the first or the second type chain, six colors with six pieces, 3/4" round. The chain or cord has been replaced with a ball. Made in the 1940s or 1950s. $30-40.

Bottom left: Ball, third type with vinyl cord, three colors with six pieces, 3/4" round. Made in the late 1960s. Hard to find. $50-60.

Bottom center: Bowling pin with ball inside, six colors with six pieces, 2" tall. Made in the 1950s. Hard to find. $60-70.

Bottom right: Bowling pin taken apart.

Bowling pin with ball inside, three colors with six pieces, 2" tall. Made in the 1950s. Hard to find. $50-60.

Football, six colors with six pieces, 1" long. Made in the 1940s. Very hard to find. $90-100.

Bowling pin, six colors with six pieces, 2 1/4" tall. Made in the 1970s. $5-10.

Football, five colors with five pieces, 1 1/4" long. Made in the 1950s. $25-35.

Man on horse back, six colors with six pieces, 2" tall x 2 1/4" long. Made in the 1960s. $15-20.

Man on horse back, six colors with six pieces, 2" tall x 2 3/8" long. Made in the 1960s. $15-20.

Man on horse back, six colors with six pieces, 2" tall x 2 3/8" long. Made in the 1960s. $15-20.

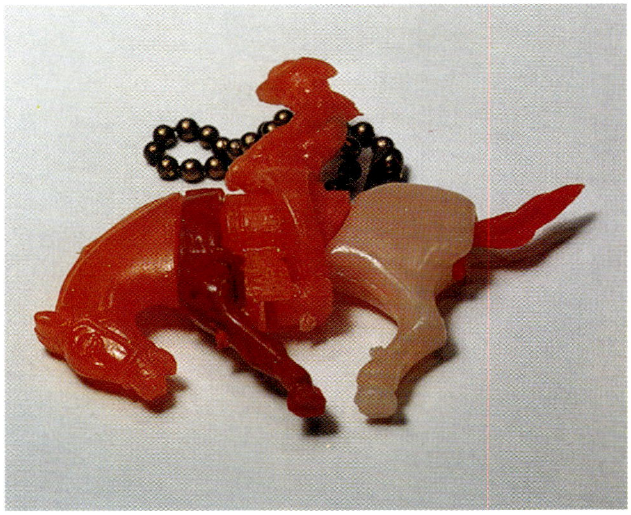

Man on bucking horse, three colors with six pieces, 2" long x 1 3/4" high. Made in Hong Kong by Fleetwood Toys Inc., NCY 10010, in the 1970s. $5-10.

Donkey rider, six colors with six pieces, 2" long x 1 3/4" high. Made in the 1940s. Hard to find. $60-70.

Covered wagon, five colors with six pieces, 2" tall x 1 5/8" long. Made in the 1950s. $30-40.

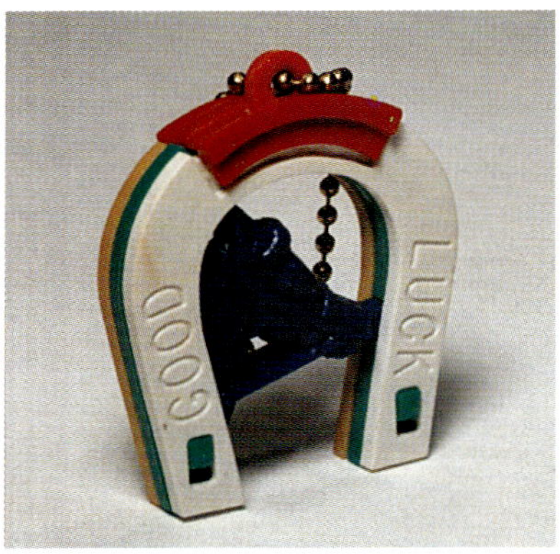

Horse shoe, six colors with six pieces, 2" tall x 1 5/8" long. Made in the 1950s. $30-40.

Scotty dog, earliest type, six colors with six pieces, 1 3/8" long x 1 1/8" high. Note: the left ear is bigger than the right ear. Made in the 1940s. Rare. $125-150.

Scotty dog, second model, six colors with six pieces, 1 3/8" long x 1 1/8" high. Note: ears are the same size. Made in the 1940s. Very hard to find. $90-100.

Elephant, six colors with six pieces, 1 1/2" long x 1" high. Made in the 1940s. Hard to find. $70-90.

Scotty dog, four colors with six pieces, 1 3/4" long x 1 1/2" high. Made in the 1950s. Hard to find. $70-80.

Scotty dog, three colors with six pieces, 1 3/4" long x 1 1/2" high. Made in the 1950s. Hard to find. $60-70.

Elephant, five colors with six pieces, 1 1/2" long x 1" high. Made in the 1940s. Hard to find. $60-70.

Elephant, four colors with six pieces, 1 1/2" long x 1" high. Made in the 1940s. Hard to find. $50-60.

Elephant, four colors with six pieces, 2" tall x 2 1/4" long. Made in the 1970s. $15-20.

Duck, five colors with five pieces, 2" tall. Made in the 1960s. $15-25.

Duck, four colors with five pieces, 2" tall. Made in the 1960s. $10-15.

Dragonfly, six colors with six pieces, 1 1/2" long. Made of vinyl in the 1970s. $2-3.

Dragon, six colors with six pieces, 2 3/4" long. Made of vinyl in the 1970s. $2-3.

Bug, six colors with six pieces, 1 3/4" long. Made of vinyl in the 1970s. $2-3.

Key chain puzzles. Made in Hong Kong for Fleetwood Toys Inc., NCY 10010, in the 1970s. $35-45.

Tak-A-Part puzzles. Made by Arkin A-Ok Products in 1991. $3-5.

Plas-Trix key chain puzzle. Made in the 1950s. $15-25.

Rubber Band Shooters

Ree Peter Gun, shoots rubber bands, 16 1/2" long. Made of wood & steel in the 1940s. Hard to find. $80-100.

Fungun, shoots rubber bands. Made of wood in the 1930s. $20-30.

Lawman's Special made of plastic by Industro Motive Corporation, Troy, Michigan 48084, in the 1970s. This Special is in the original package and is hard to find. $60-80.

Rubber Band Gun, 7 1/2" long. Made of plastic by Cadaco Ellis in Chicago, Illinois. $20-30.

Rubber Band Gun. Patent # 2578198, No. 100. Made of plastic by Auto-Band in the 1950s. $20-30.

Luger - 45 Rubber Band Gun, 8" long. Made of plastic. $15-20.

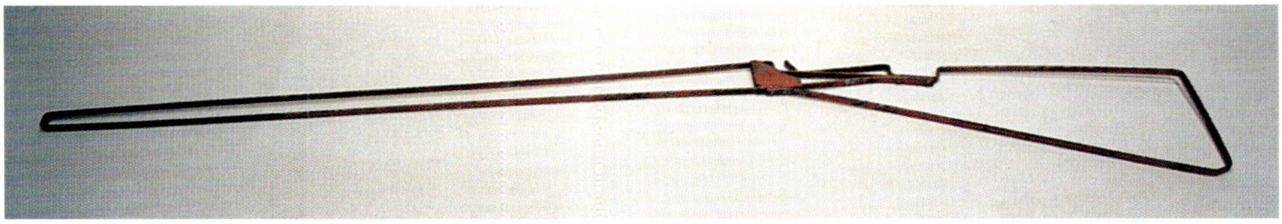

Rubber Band Rifle, 28 1/4" long. Made of wire steel in the 1930s. Rare. $80-100.

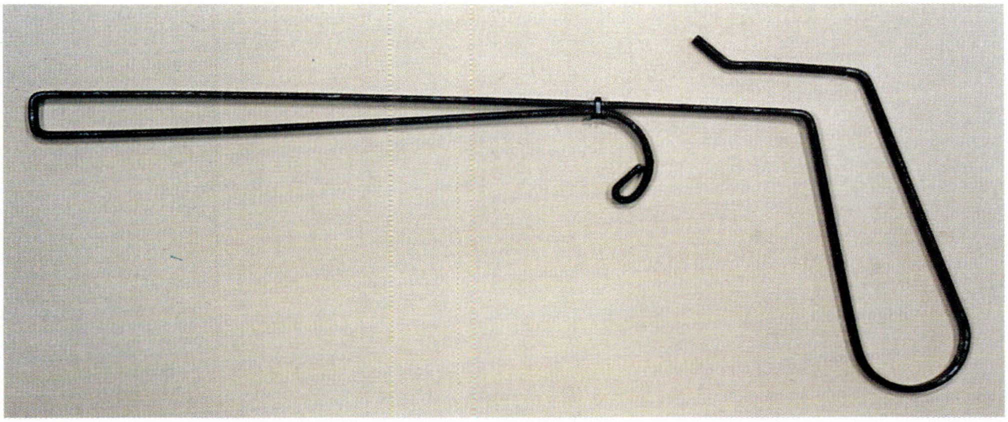

Rubber Band Pistol, 9 1/2" long. Made of wire steel in the 1930s. Rare. $60-80.

Squirt Guns

USA Liquid Pistol, 5" long. Made of cast iron by Parker Stearns in 1896. $125-175.

Wizard, 5" long. Made of cast iron by Parker Stearns in 1896. $125-175.

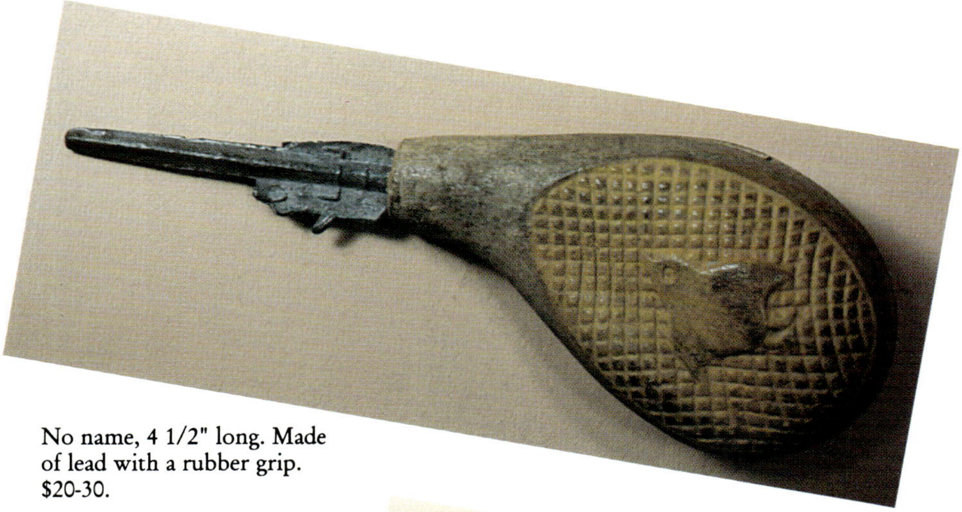

No name, 4 1/2" long. Made of lead with a rubber grip. $20-30.

No name, 5 1/4" long. Made of lead with a rubber grip in the U.S.A. by M & L. $40-50.

No name, 5" long. Made of lead with a rubber grip in the U.S.A. by M & L. $40-50.

No name, 4 3/4" long. Made of lead with a rubber grip in Japan. $20-30.

No. 71 Water Pistol, 5 1/4" long. Patent # 1662067. Made of steel in 1928. $50-60.

Daisy No. 8, 5 1/2" long. Made of steel by the Daisy MFG.Co., Plymouth, Michigan. Patented on June 22, 1915. $60-80.

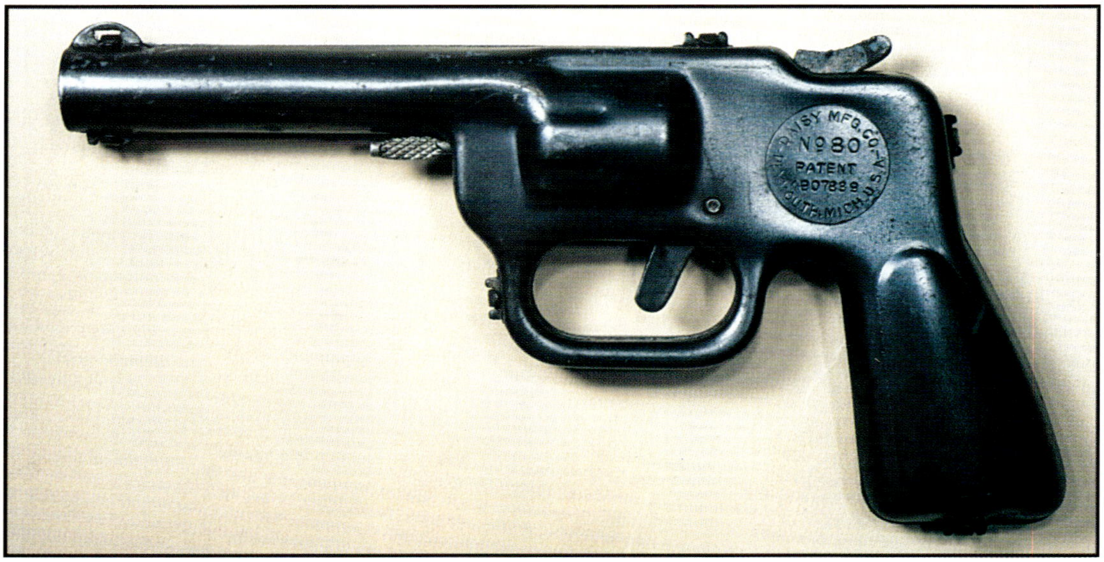

Daisy No. 80, 7" long. Patent # 1907839. Made of steel by the Daisy MFG.Co., Plymouth, Michigan, in 1931. $60-80.

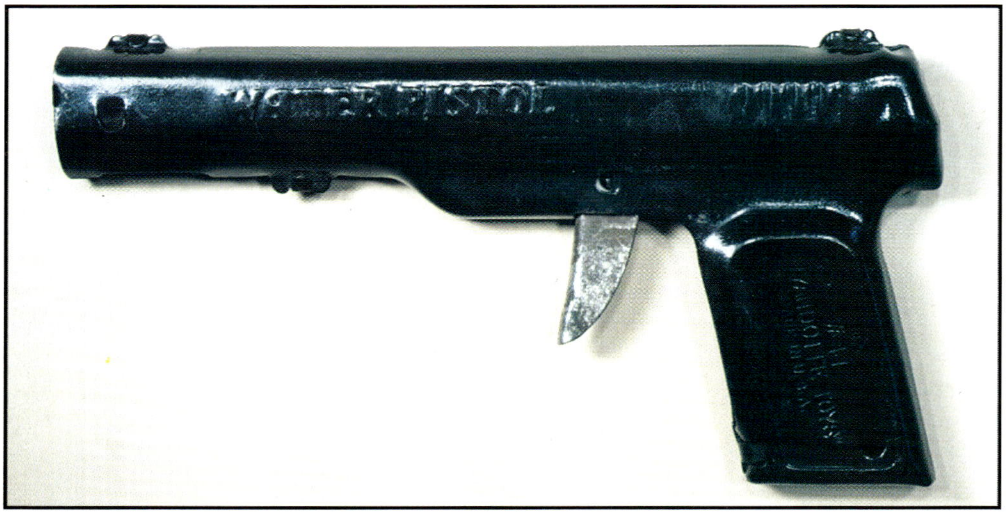

Water Pistol # 41, 6 3/4" long. Made of steel by Wyandotte Toys. $40-50.

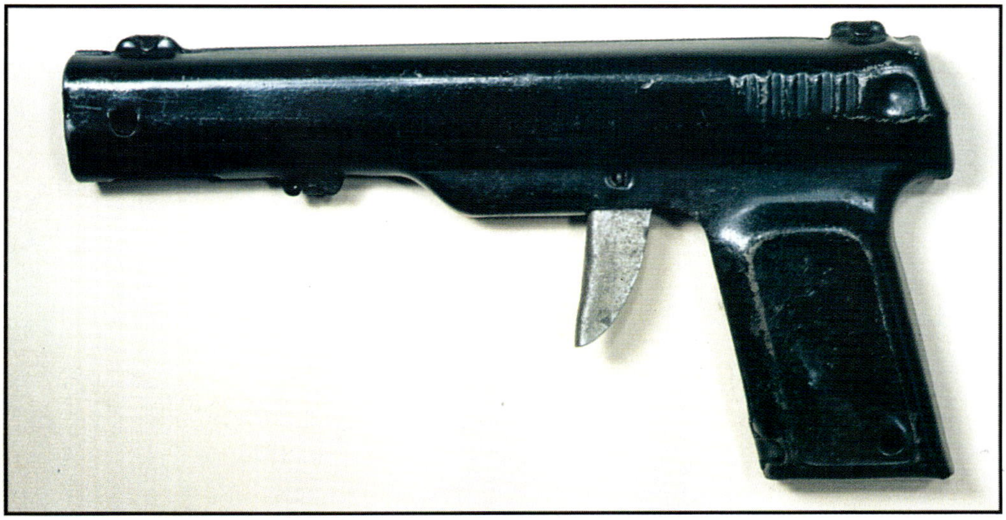

No name, 6 3/4" long. Made of steel. This is the same as the Water Pistol # 41 by Wyandotte Toys, unmarked. $30-40.

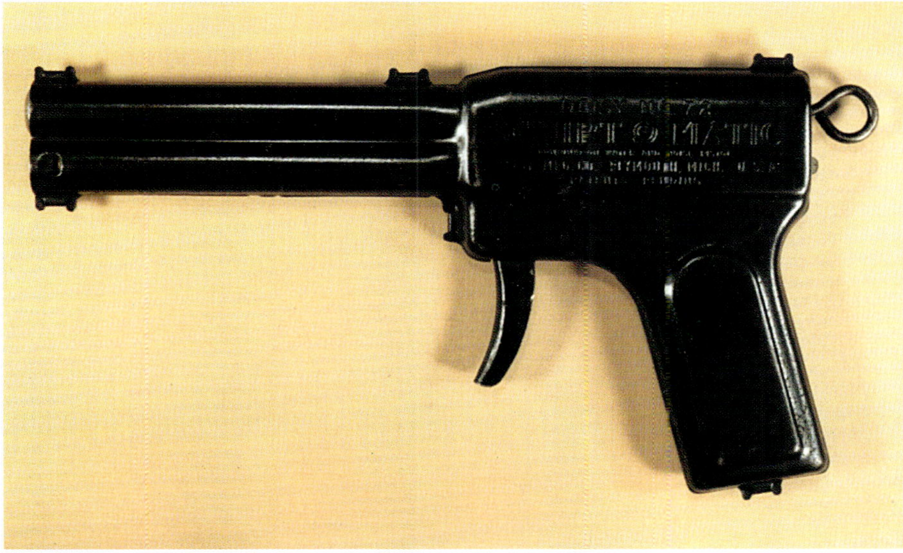

Daisy No. 72, squirt and pop gun, 8 1/2" long. Made of steel by the Daisy MFG.Co., Plymouth, Michigan. $80-100.

No name water pistol, 4" long. Made of tin and brass. $10-20.

Ring squirter, 2" long. Made of lead with a rubber grip in Japan in the 1950s. $10-20.

Power-Jet Squad Gun, 30 1/2" long. Made of plastic by Mattel Inc. This is a squirt gun and a cap gun made in the 1950s. Very hard to find. $150-200.

Squirt gun in the original box, 4 1/2" long. Came in assorted colors. Made of plastic with a brass tip by Kilgore, Westerville, Ohio, in the 1950s. $40-60.

Squirt gun, 4 1/2" long. Came in assorted colors: blue, red, green, or black. $20-30 each.

250 Repeater, 4 3/4" long. Came in assorted colors. Made of plastic with a brass tip by Park Plastic, New Jersey, in the 1950s. $30-40.

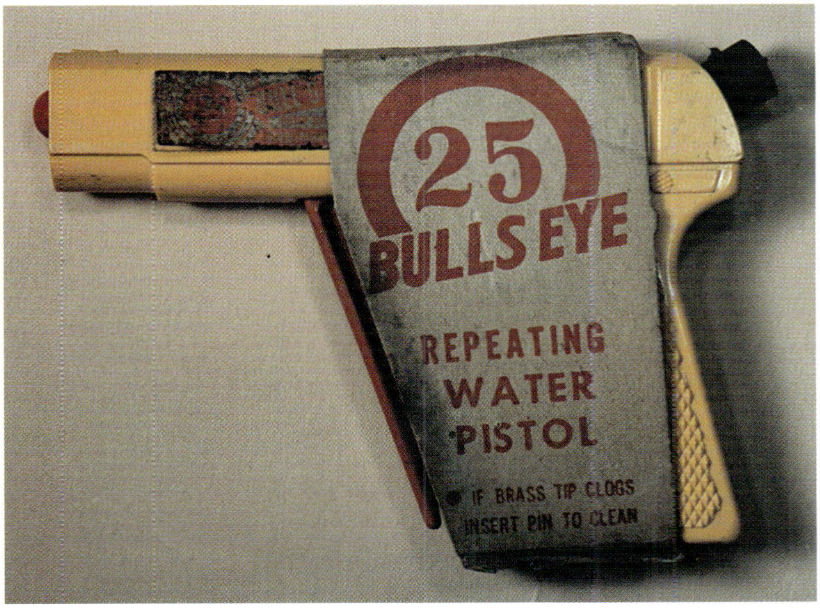

Bullseye 25 in the original box, 4 1/2" long. Came in assorted colors. Made of plastic with a plastic tip by Tops Plastic Inc., New York, New York, in the 1950s. Note: it says "if brass tip clogs insert pin to clean." This gun has a plastic tip, not brass. $60-70.

Tiny squirt gun with the original tag, 4" long. Made of plastic with a plastic tip by Irwin Corp., Fitchburg, Massachusetts, in the 1950s. $40-50.

Super Jet with the original box, 7" long. Made of plastic with a brass tip by Knickerbocker, Hollywood, California, in the 1950s. $60-70.

Luger original box. Made by Park Plastic, New Jersey, in the 1950s. $20-30.

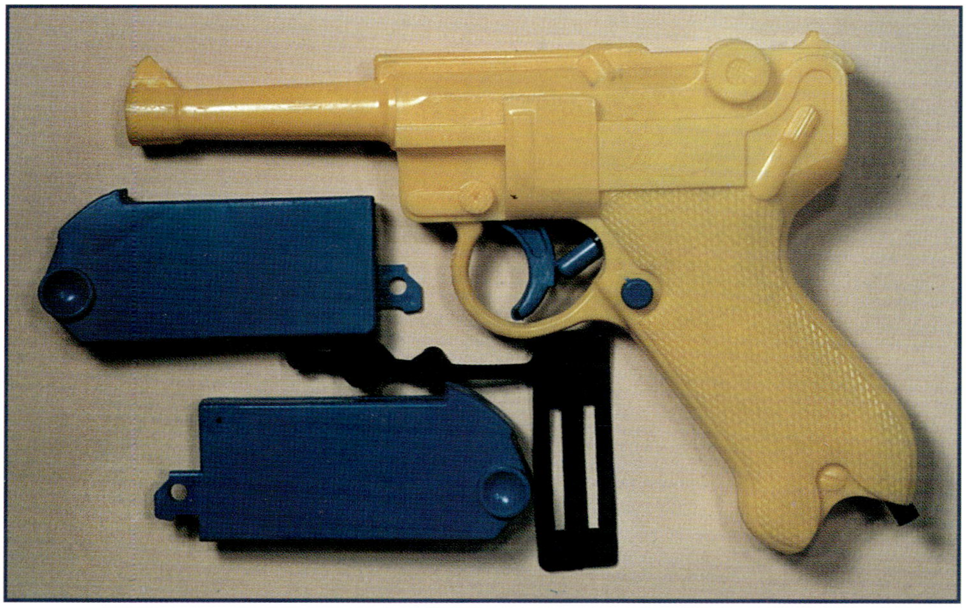

Luger, with refillable water clips, 7" long. Came in assorted colors. Made of plastic with a plastic tip by Park Plastic, New Jersey, in the 1950s. $125-150.

Luger, 8" long. Made of plastic with a plastic tip by Knickerbocker, Hollywood, California, in 1955. $30-40.

Luger in the original box, 7" long. Came in assorted colors. Made of plastic with a plastic tip by Ideal Novelty and Toys Company of Hollis 7, New York, in the 1950s. $60-80.

Luger, 7" long. Came in assorted colors. Made of plastic with a plastic tip by Park Plastic, New Jersey, in the 1960s. 10-20.

No name, 5 3/4" long. Plastic with a brass tip. $15-20.

Par-Kee, 2 3/4" long. Made of plastic with a plastic tip by Park Plastic, New Jersey, in the 1960s. $10-15.

Caliber 25 Automatic Pistol No.623, 4 1/4" long. Plastic with a plastic tip. $5-10.

Squirt ring, 2 1/2" long. Made of vinyl in the 1980s. $1-2.

Bull Dog squirt shooter, 3 1/2" long. No.3321. Made of plastic in China in the 1990s. $1-2.

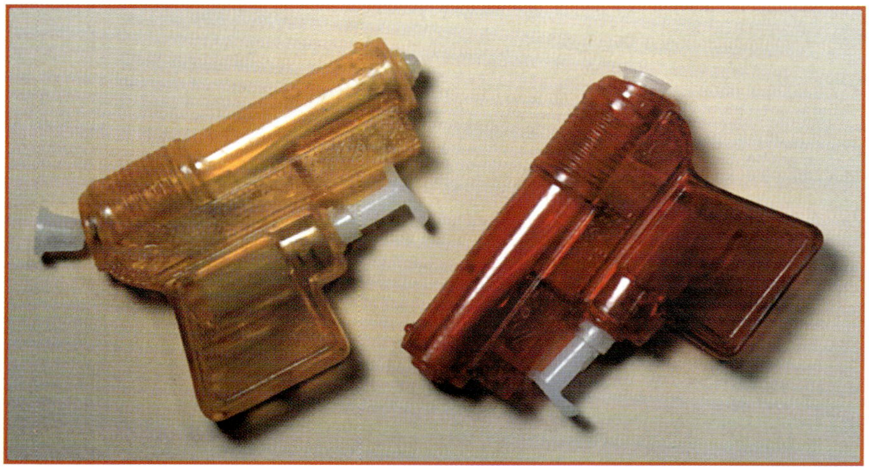

No name, 2 5/8" long. Made of plastic in China. $1-2.

Dragnet, 4 3/4" long. Came in assorted colors. Made of plastic with a brass tip in the 1960s. $60-80.

Lunar Ray, 7" long. Came in assorted colors. Made of plastic with a plastic tip in the 1960s. $80-90.

Watermatic Camera Squirter. Made of plastic in the 1990s. $3-4.

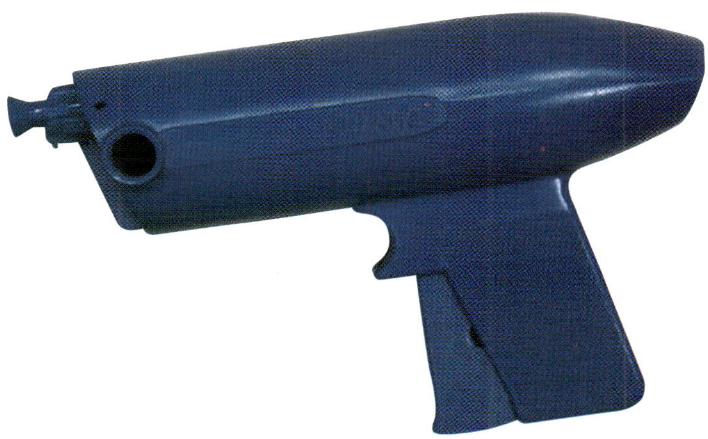

Bubbl-matic, 7" long. Shoots bubbles. Made of plastic by Kenner in the 1960s. $20-30.

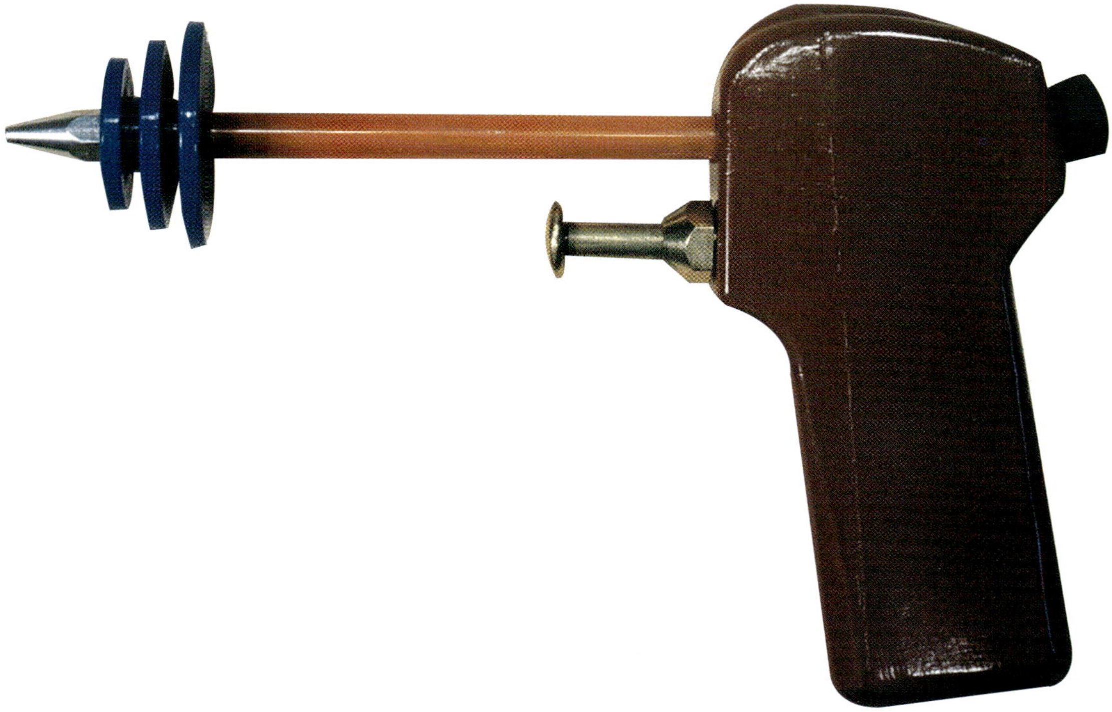

Atom-Matic Water Rocket, earliest type, 7" long. Made of die-cast brass and plastic. This type has an orange plastic covered brass barrel with an aluminum nozzle and a blue plastic end. Made by Playcraft Company, Skokie, Illinois, in the 1940s. Rare. $800-900.

Atom-Matic Water Rocket, second type, 7" long. Made of die-cast aluminum, brass, and plastic. This type has a blue plastic covered aluminum barrel with an aluminum nozzle and a red plastic end. Made by Playcraft Company, Skokie, Illinois, in the 1940s. Hard to find. $700-800.

Atom-Matic Water Rocket original box. Made by Playcraft Company, Skokie, Illinois, in the 1940s. Very hard to find. Box only: $75-100.

Space Jet, 7" long. Made of plastic with a brass tip by Renwal, # 193, in the 1950s. Hard to find. $300-400. *Courtesy of Janet M. Dundas.*

Space Gun, 5 1/2" long. Made of plastic with a brass tip in the 1950s. $200-300.

T.K. No. 6821, 6 3/4" long. Made of plastic with a plastic tip in China in the 1990s. $20-30.

Squirt Ray, original display box with 25 assorted guns. Made by Park Plastic, New Jersey, in the 1950s. $1000-1200.

Squirt Ray, 5 1/2" long. Came in assorted colors. Made of plastic with a brass tip by Park Plastic, New Jersey, in the 1950s. $50-60 each.

No name, 5 1/2" long. This model looks somewhat like the Squirt Ray. It has a plastic tip and was made in Hong Kong. $30-40.

No name, 5 1/2" long. Made of plastic with a plastic tip. $30-40.

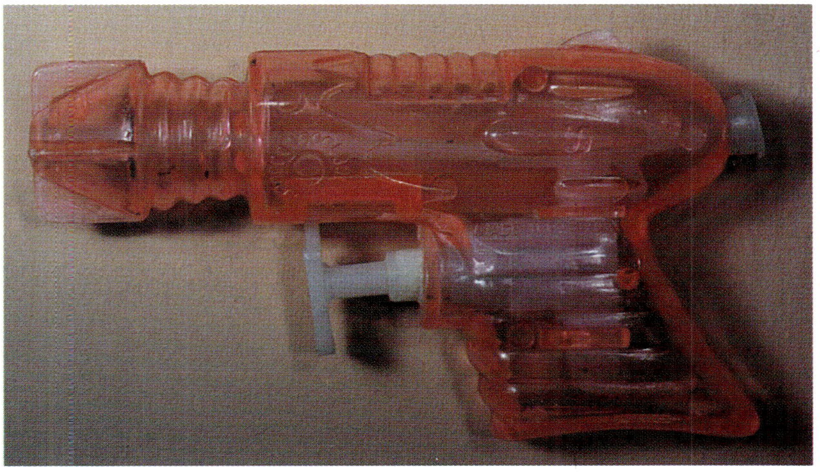

No name, 4" long. Came in assorted colors. Made of plastic with a plastic tip in Taiwan. $30-40.

Park, 4 1/2" long. Came in assorted colors. Made of plastic with a plastic tip in Singapore for Park Plastic, New Jersey. $30-40.

No name, 5 1/2" long. Patent # 2707579. Made of plastic with a plastic tip by Palmer in 1955. $200-300.

Polythene water pistol in the original bag, 5" long. Made of vinyl with a plastic tip in Hong Kong. $30-40.

Water Gun, 3 3/4" long. Made of plastic with a plastic tip by Palmer Plastics in the 1950s. $30-40.

Wee Gee, 2 3/4" long. All black, made of plastic with a brass tip by Park Plastic, New Jersey, in the 1950s and 1960s. $30-40.

Wee Gee, 2 3/4" long. Black and white, made of plastic with a brass tip by Park Plastic, New Jersey, in the 1950s and 1960s. $30-40.

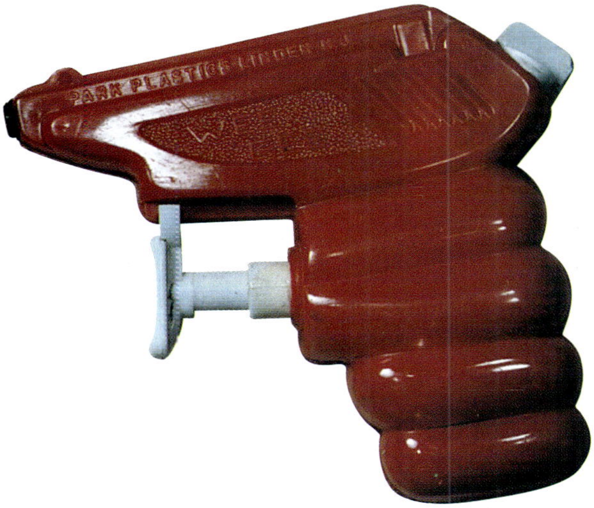

Dee Gee, 2 3/4" long. All black, made of plastic with two brass tips by Park Plastic, New Jersey, in the 1950s and 1960s. $30-40.

Wee Gee, 2 3/4" long. Red and white, made of plastic with a brass tip by Park Plastic, New Jersey, in the 1950s and 1960s. $40-50.

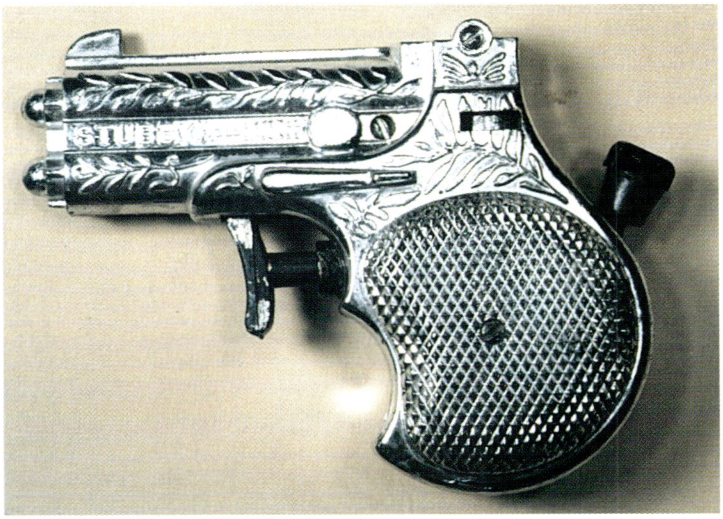

Stubby, 3 3/4" long. Patent # 2724528. Made of plastic with a plastic tip by Knickerbocker, Hollywood, California, in 1955. $30-40.

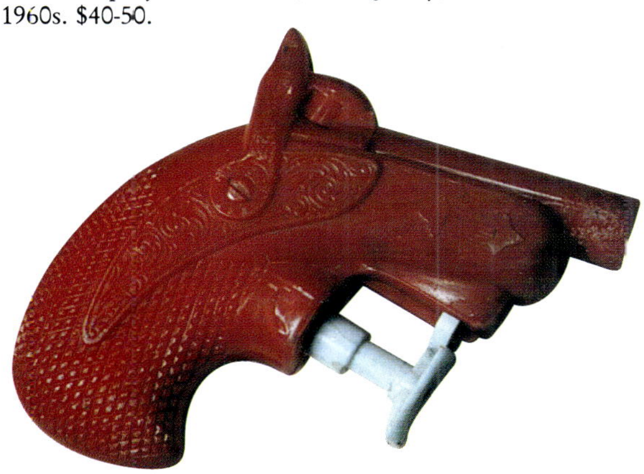

No name, 3 1/4" long. Made of plastic with a plastic tip by Park Plastic, New Jersey, in the 1960s. $30-40.

Fanning Water Gun in the original bag, 10" long. Made of plastic with a plastic tip by Park Plastic, New Jersey, in the 1960s. Hard to find. $150-200.

Junior Ranger with the original box, 8 1/2" long. Made of plastic with a brass tip by Premier Plastic Company, New York, in the 1950s. $100-125.

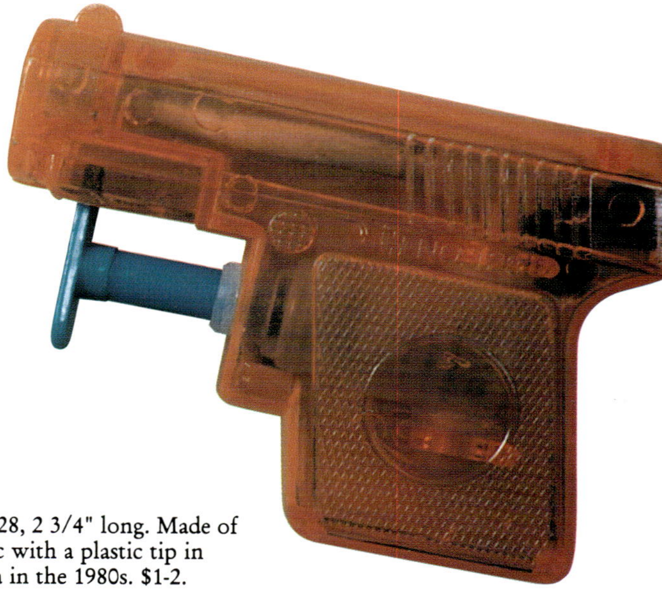

HT 128, 2 3/4" long. Made of plastic with a plastic tip in China in the 1980s. $1-2.

Western Squirt Water Pistol No. 202 in the original box, 7 1/2" long. Made of plastic with a brass tip by Kilgor Company in the 1950s. Hard to find. $200-250.

No name, 3 1/4" long. Made of plastic with a plastic tip by NK in China in the 1980s. $1-2.

No. 2143, 3 1/2" long. Made of plastic with a plastic tip in Hong Kong. $1-2.

No name, 5 1/2" long. Made of plastic with a plastic tip by MM. $1-2.

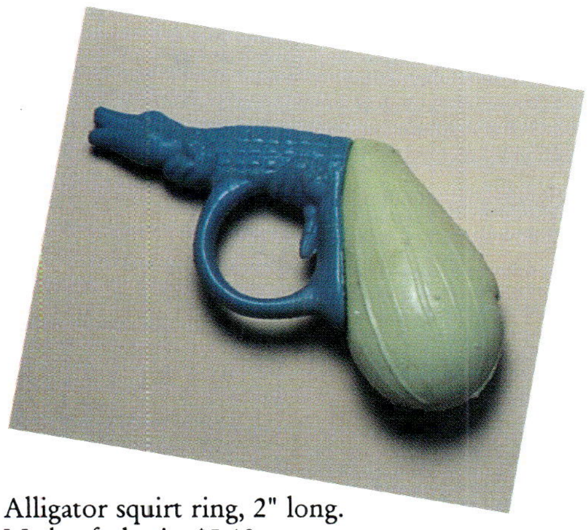

Alligator squirt ring, 2" long. Made of plastic. $5-10.

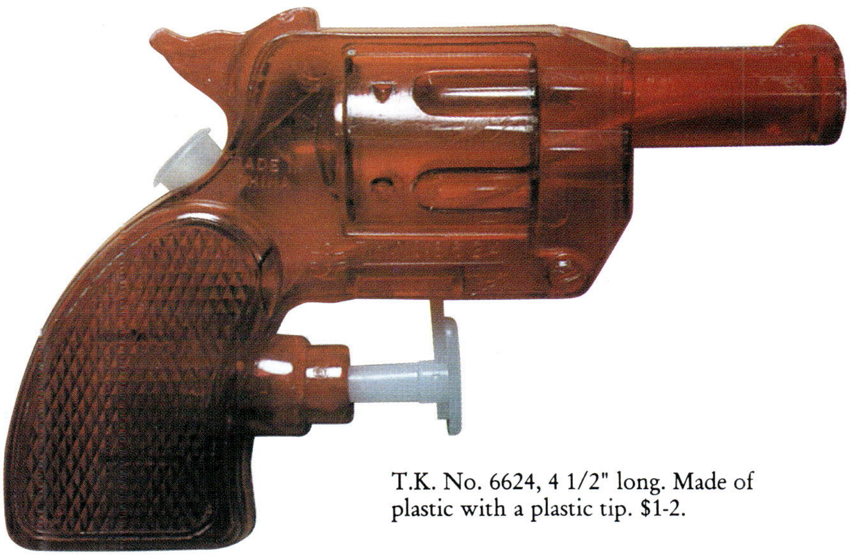

T.K. No. 6624, 4 1/2" long. Made of plastic with a plastic tip. $1-2.

Mighty Mite Water Shooting Machine Gun with the original box, 13" long. Made of plastic with a brass tip by Arliss, 369 DeKalb Avenue, Brooklyn 5, New York, in the 1950s. Hard to find. $100-150.

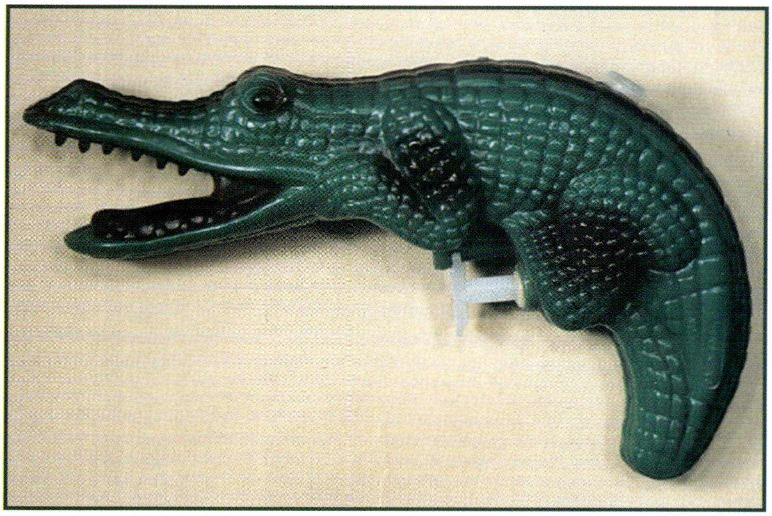

Alligator, 6" long. Made of plastic with a plastic tip in Hong Kong, # 721, in the 1960s. $30-40. *Courtesy of Bob and Connie MacKinnon.*

Brass knuckle design, 3 3/4" long. Made of plastic with a plastic tip for Barton in Hong Kong. $20-30.

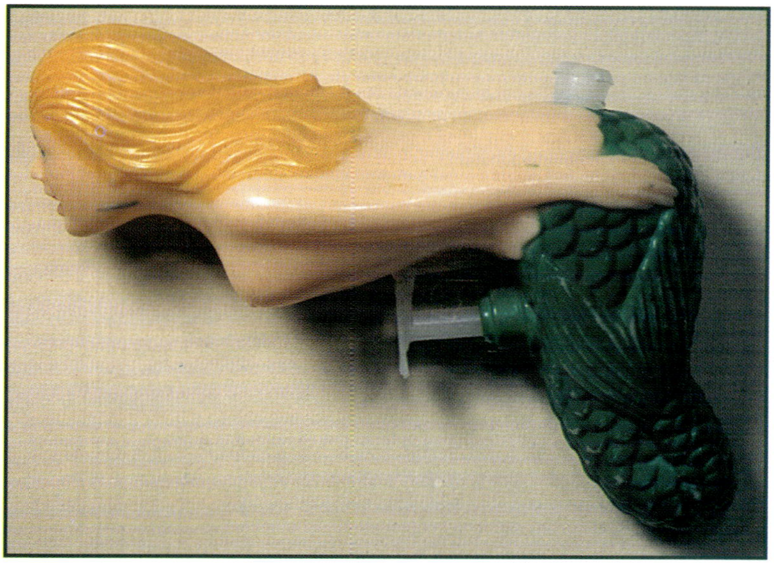

Mermaid No. 734, 4 1/4" long. Made of plastic with a plastic tip in Hong Kong in the 1960s. $30-40. *Courtesy of Mearl and May Noftz.*

Oil Can. This brass oil can made a great water shooter in the 1940s and 1950s. $30-40.

No name, 2 1/2" long. Made of plastic with a plastic tip by Irwin Corporation, Fitchburg, Massachusetts, in the 1950s. $10-20.

Water gun, 6 1/2" long. Made of plastic with a plastic tip by Harben Plastic Company in the 1950s. $20-30.

Squirt nickel. Note the small hole in the center of the O in "United States of America." Made in the 1950s. $10-20.

No name, 7 3/4" long. Made of steel. $20-30.

Squirt nickel, other side.

Squirt Pen in the original package. It shoots disappearing ink. Made in the 1950s. $10-20.

Bird squirt shooter No. 151, 3 1/2" long. Made of plastic in China in 1990. $1-2.

Bubble Gun, 8 1/4" long. Made of plastic by Atomic Ind., 2044 North 3rd Street, Milwaukee 12, Wisconsin, in the 1960s. $20-30.

Water Force, 7 3/4" long. Made of plastic in China for Placo toys. This water gun has a pump in the handle to create air pressure to shoot the water. Although this water gun was made in the 1990s, if you put it away for 30 years it will be worth much more than today's price of $3-5.

Things That Shoot

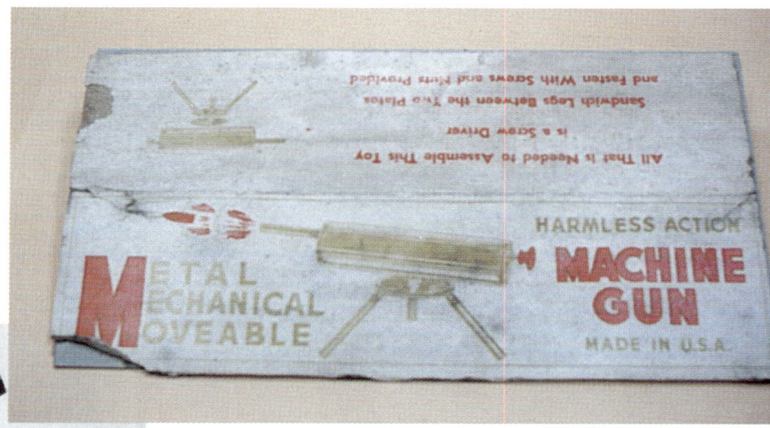

Machine gun box only: $10-20.

Machine gun with the original box, 13 3/4" long x 7 1/2" high. Made of tin and shoots wooden bullets. Made in the U.S.A. by an unknown maker around the 1940s. $80-100.

Cannon, 14" long. Shoots plastic bullets. Made of plastic and vinyl by Marx in the 1960s. $50-60.

Cannon, 9 3/4" long. Shoots 1/4" round plastic balls. Made of tin by Buddy L in the 1960s. $60-80.

Cannon N. 200, 5" long. Shoots wooden balls. Made of die cast metal by Manoil in the 1940s. $30-40.

Cannon, 4" long. Shoots BBs. Made of cast iron with rubber wheels by Arcade in the 1930s. $80-100.

Pea shooter and bean blower. The pea shooters have an inside diameter of 1/4"; the bean shooters have an inside diameter of 5/16". Made of plastic by Serv-A-Toy, R. Sitterly, Norwalk, Ohio, in the 1950s. $30-40.

Cannon, 5" long. Made of die cast metal in England. $15-20.

Fire Cracker Cannon. Shoots 1 1/4" balls. The base is 3 7/8" long x 2 1/2" wide and the barrel is 2" long x 1 3/8". Made of cast iron by Kilgore in the 1920s. Hard to find. $175-225.

Wonder Target Peas by Chemical Sundries, Chicago 50, Illinois, in 1954. $10-20.

Krest Pea and Pellet Shooter box.

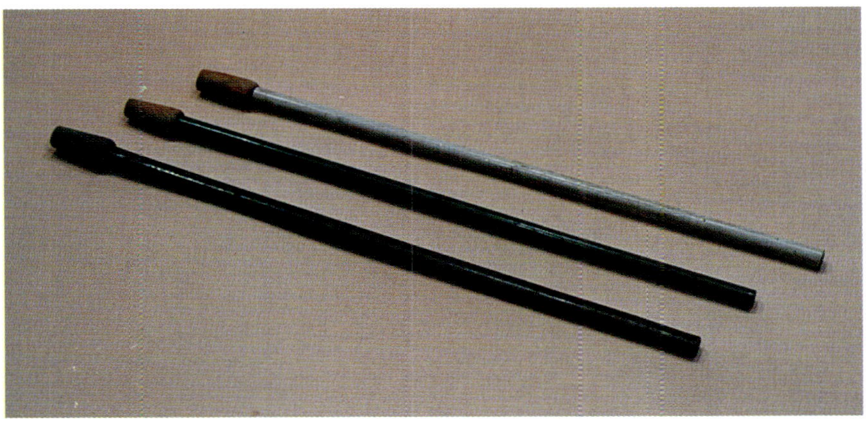

Pea shooters, 12" long with an inside diameter of 1/4". Came in assorted colors. Made of painted steel with a wooden tip in the 1930s. $40-50.

Krest Pea and Pellet Shooter, 5" long. Made of tin by Krest in the 1950s. $40-50.

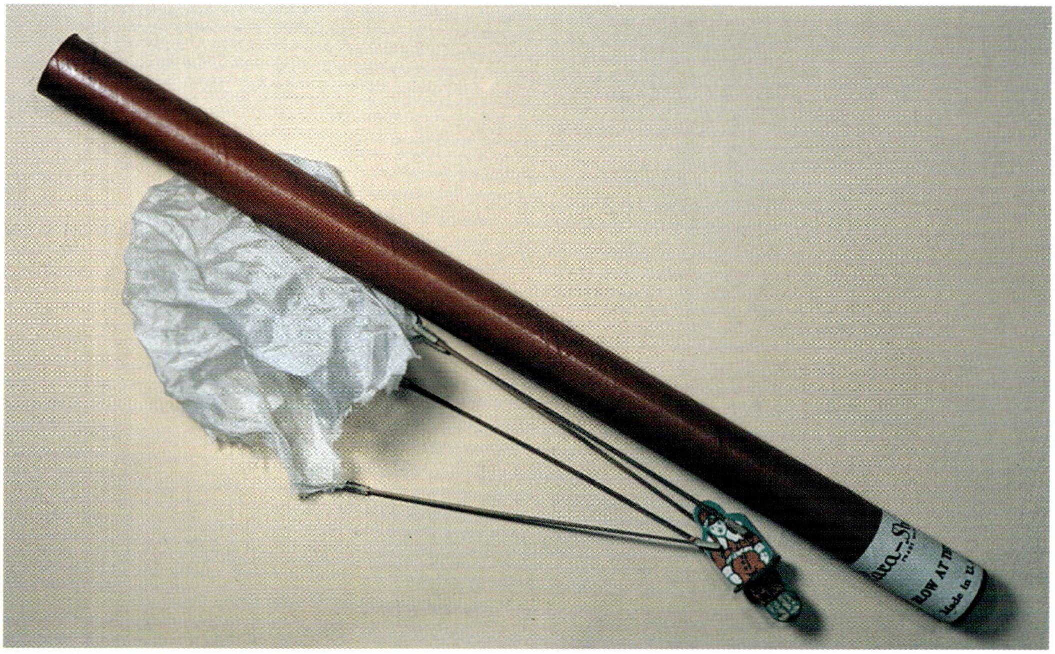

Para-Shooter, the earliest type with bamboo parachute lines. The tube is 11" long. Made of cardboard in the U.S.A. in the late 1940s. Very hard to find. $80-100.

Para-Shooter, the second type with plastic parachute lines. The tube is 11" long and is made of cardboard. Made in the U.S.A. in the early 1950s. Hard to find. $60-80.

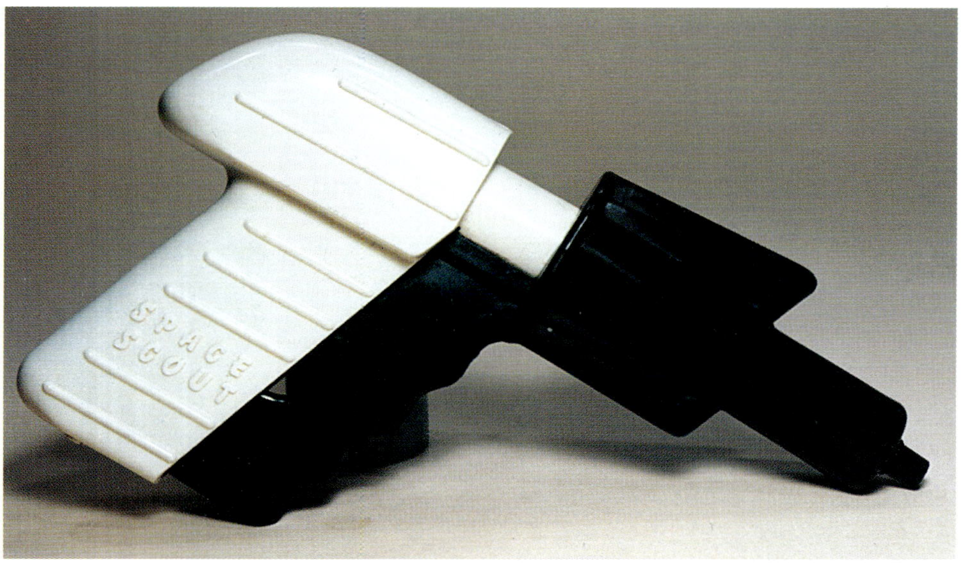

Space Scout Potato Gun, 6 3/4" long. Shoots potato pellets. Made of plastic in the 1950s. $30-40.

Potato Gun with the original box, 6 3/4" long. Shoots potato pellets. Made of plastic in Hong Kong in the 1960s. $20-30.

Topper cane, D.L.R., No. 8003, 30" long. Shoots plastic bullets. Made of plastic by D.L.R. of Elizabeth, New Jersey, in 1966. $60-80.

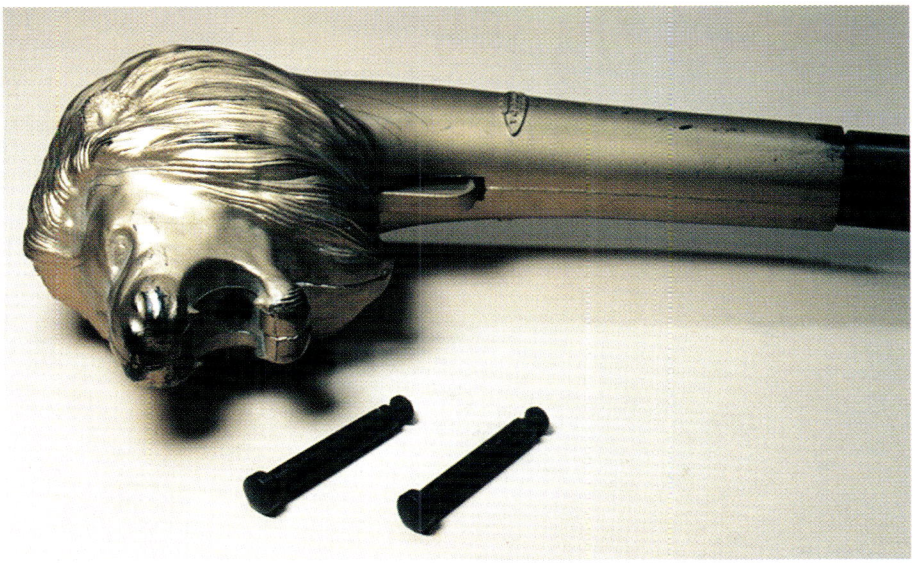

Topper cane, lions head and plastic bullets.

Topper cane, bottom storage for bullets.

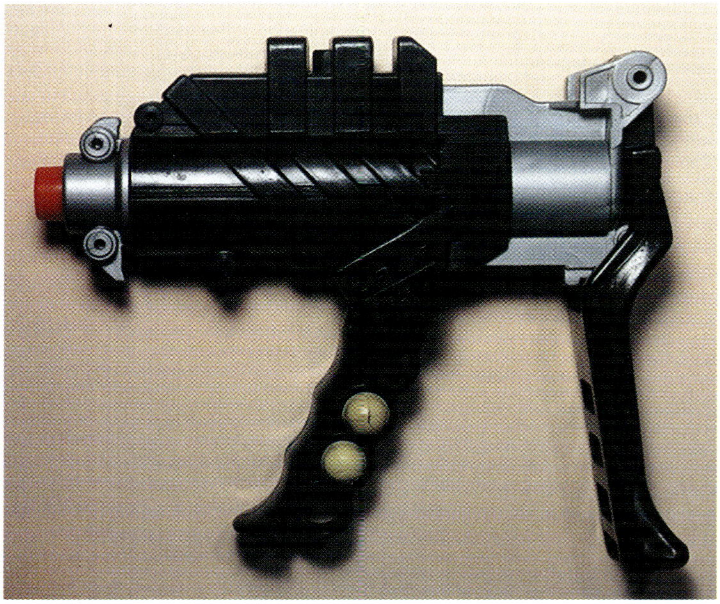

Larami plastic gun, 5 1/2" long. Shcots rubber bullet. Made in 1986. $10-15.

Target Game, 9" long. Shoots plastic bullets. Made of wood with a steel barrel by Evanston Mfg. Co., Detroit 5, Michigan, in the 1950s. $50-60.

Brabo plastic ball shooter, 3 1/2" long. Made of plastic in Hong Kong in the 1960s. $5-10.

Thompson submachine gun model 1921, shoots plastic balls, 34 1/2" long. Made of plastic in Japan in the 1980s. Note that this is a kit. $150-200.

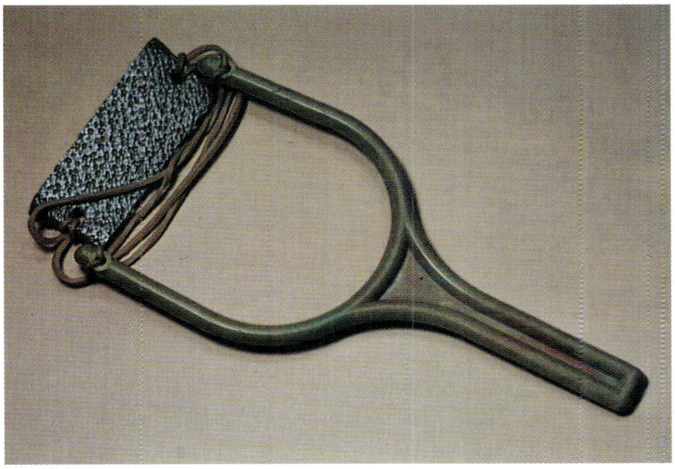

Slingshot, 6" long. Made of plastic in the late 1940s and the early 1950s. $15-20.

Sharp Shooter slingshot with the original package, 6 1/4" long. Made of steel in Japan in the 1950s. $30-40.

Slingshot, 6" long. Made of plastic in the late 1940s and the early 1950s. $15-20.

Slingshot, 5 1/2" long. Made of steel. $10-15.

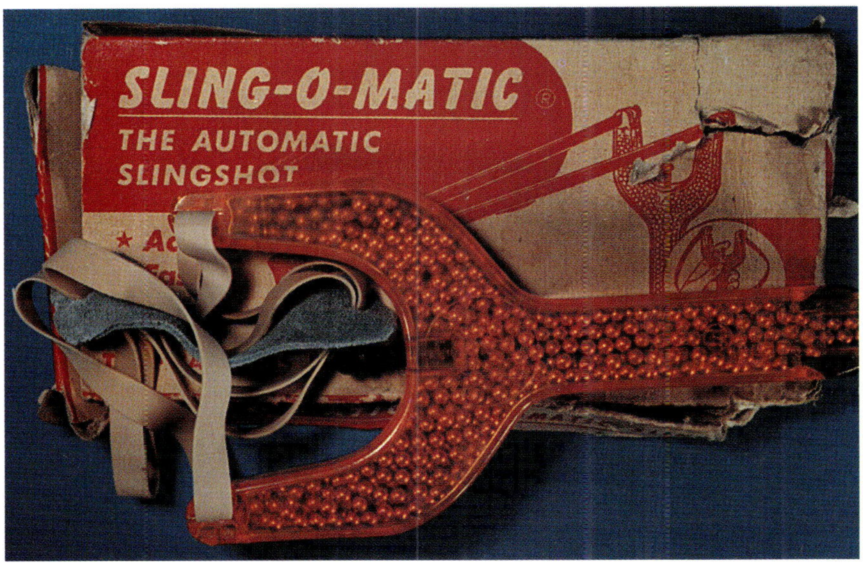

Sling-O-Matic slingshot with the original box, 7 1/2" x 3 5/8" x 3/4". To remove a BB, press the brass plunger down. Made of plastic by Tropical Sales, Box 35, Coconut Grove Station, Miami 33, Florida. $80-100.

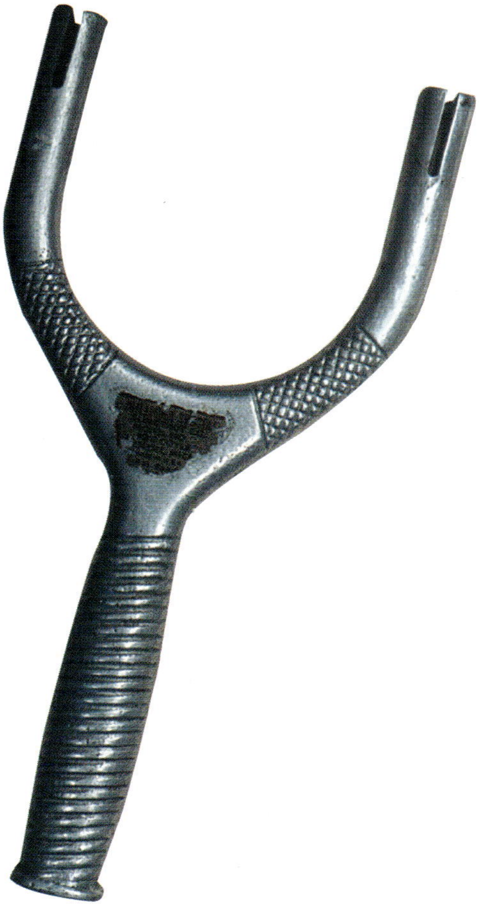

Milligan Special Model No. 1 slingshot, 7 3/4" long. Made of aluminum by Milligan Slingshot Company, 9962 Coyle, Detroit, Michigan, in the 1940s. $30-40.

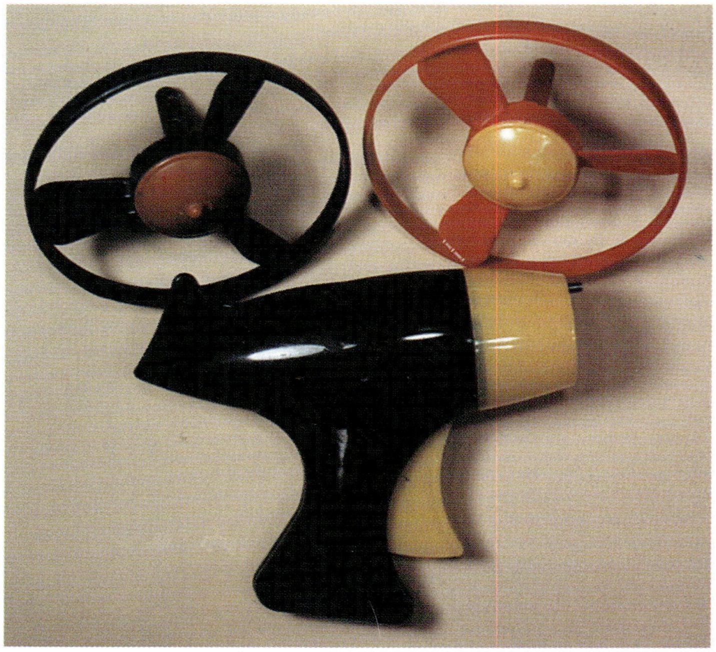

Flying Saucer Gun, 4 1/2" long. Shoots tops. Made of plastic by the U.S. Plastic Company, 2570 East Walnut, Pasadena 8, California, in the 1950s. $60-80.

Plastic Flying Saucer in the original bag, 3 3/4" long. Shoots flying saucer. Made of plastic in Hong Kong, No. 492, in the 1960s. $10-15.

Flying Saucer Guns original box.